HOLIDAY WALKS
in
NORMANDY

Judy Smith

Published by Sigma Leisure – an imprint of Sigma Press, 1 South Oak Lane, Wilmslow, Cheshire SK9 6AR, England.

British Library Cataloguing in Publication Data
A CIP record for this book is available from the British Library.

ISBN: 1-85058-736-1

Typesetting and Design by: Sigma Press, Wilmslow, Cheshire.

Cover design by: The Agency, Macclesfield, Cheshire.

Printed by: MFP Design & Print

Cover Photographs: Main: The cliffs of Étretat. Small (left to right): Château Gaillard near les Andelys; Lobster pots on the Îles Chausey; In the village of le Bec Hellouin.

Photographs: the author

Maps: Michael Gilbert

Thanks - to the very helpful staff of Offices de Tourisme all over Normandy.

DISCLAIMER

The footpaths of Normandy

Normandy is a jewel with many facets. It is a rich agricultural country producing cheese and cream, cider and calvados, a place where the grass really is greener (it is certainly said to be), where speckled cows graze contentedly under laden apple trees in the orchards of colourful half-timbered farms. It is also a region steeped in history and religion, where ancient abbeys and monasteries conceal themselves in every river valley and each village seems to have a church of architectural note. The talents of its writers and artists are well-known – Flaubert and Maupassant were enthusiastic in describing their native land, and Monet and his school of impressionists were inspired to produce many paintings of the chalk cliffs and the Seine valley. It is a land of fine horses – trotters and thoroughbreds have been raised on the green swards of Normandy for many generations, while those magnificent draught horses, the percherons, are bred in the south. On the darker side, Normandy is a country that has seen many conflicts, a country that in recent times has proudly paid a high price for the freedom of the western world.

Many of you reading this book will have visited Normandy before – it is, after all, 'just across the channel', the arrival point from which to set out on a journey to the Dordogne or the Côte d'Azur. In the last few years, it has become so accessible with hovercraft, shuttle and new road links that it is now a popular destination for a weekend or a short break. Even if you have previously spent some time in Normandy, this book should offer you something quite different. Exploring on foot brings you closer to the land and its people, and takes you to beauty spots and viewpoints that you could never hope to reach by car. The selection of walks here is intended to provide for all tastes and abilities, from short family strolls along the coast to all-day hikes in the forested hills. The routes are all circular, so that you will have no transport problems, and they range from 2½ to 14 miles in length. Many have possible short cuts or extensions, making them even more adaptable. In addition to the main descriptions, there are suggestions for at least a hundred more routes – enough to keep you busy for quite some time. But before you set out, here are just a few words about what you will find on foot in Normandy.

The most exciting thing about walking in Normandy is the enormous contrast it offers. Geologically speaking, Normandy is divided into two parts – *Haute-Normandie* (Upper Normandy), the limestone area to the north and east, and *Basse-Normandie* (Lower Normandy) to the south and west, where the granite rock is an extension of the Armorican Massif of Brittany. This division immediately explains the differences in coastline. In the east, between Le Tréport and Le Havre, there are some remarkable white chalk cliffs towering high above beaches of rounded pebbles. A Grande Randonnée follows the coast all the way – 120km – but if that's too far, there is a splendid walk at

Criel along the highest cliffs in France, and the classic walk at Étretat takes you past the arches and needle on this most famous stretch of coastline. In total contrast are the sloping granite cliffs on the north of the Cotentin peninsula. This wild and lonely coast makes for superb walking – you can follow the narrow path along the gorse-clad cliffs at the Nez de Jobourg and look out across the remote bay of Ecalgrain to the distant Channel Islands. In between these two very different coastlines are shores of yet another kind. Here are the wide stretches of sand that were once the famous landing beaches of D-Day. Again, a coastal path will take you past all the well-known sites and memorials, and there are suggestions for a day's expedition here. But the simple circular walk at Arromanches will give you the best views of the bay, still with the remains of its mulberry harbour. One coastal walk with a difference – and one that should not be missed - is that on the Îles Chaussey. This galaxy of tiny islands off the west coast is a miniature paradise, where palm trees overlook the turquoise waters and the rise of tide is higher than anywhere in Europe.

Inland there is even more variety. In the south are the forests – Andaines and Écouves – and the particularly lovely forest of Bellême deserves special mention. Heading north there is the Suisse Normande, Normandy's prime walking country – and although the parallel with Switzerland is a little extreme, you can enjoy some fantastic views from the top of the Pain de Sucre and the Roche d'Oëtre. Farther north again, there is a totally different scene on the vast marshlands of the Cotentin, where storks are summer visitors that come here to nest. Then there is the farming region of the Auge, the home of Normandy's delicious cheeses and cider apples, and last, but not at all least, the valley of the Seine. Here you can visit Monet's house at Giverny and take a walk on the slopes above the river, or climb from Les Andelys to get the best views of the impressive Château Gaillard. This is also a region of many monasteries – catch the strains of plainsong as you pass the Abbey of St. Wandrille or arrive as did the monks of old, on a track through the woods at le Bec Hellouin.

Normandy offers so many excellent walks that making the choice for this book has been extremely difficult. To include as many good walks as possible, a 'More Walks' section has been provided with every route described. From this, you may well find favourites of your own. If you are planning to stay in an area, the More Walks section should give you ideas for at least a week's walking. The maps and leaflets suggested can all be found in the local Office de Tourisme – and you can get at least a little help with the French text from the 'Dictionary of walking words' at the back of this book. Tourist Offices in France are generally far more geared to walking than they are in England, and they will readily help with any request for information. In addition, they carry a wealth of literature on other attractions in the area – oddly, it seems to me that the smaller and more rural the office, the more well supplied and helpful it is! With each walk, a few suggestions have been included – the list of these is by no means comprehensive, but just a personal selection of places that may particularly appeal to walkers.

My heartiest thanks go to my husband Eric for his part in this book. Together we walked all the routes – and most warranted a second visit. Although we could not cover every route in the More Walks section as well, we attempted at least to visit each one. A whole year and a couple of pairs of boots have been expended in the process! But we have some splendid memories of Normandy – springtime in the Val de Saire where every bank is scattered with primroses, summer beside the Seine, the first touches of autumn in the deep forests of the south. And maybe you too will be lucky enough to witness the evening sun sinking into the western sea over the lonely Bay of Vauville. This has been an enjoyable year, and I hope you will gain as much pleasure as we have had from these fine walks. Good luck on your journey!

Judy Smith

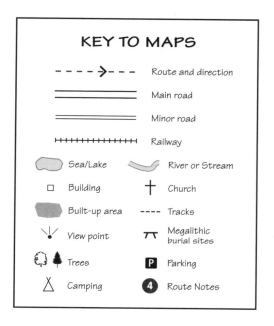

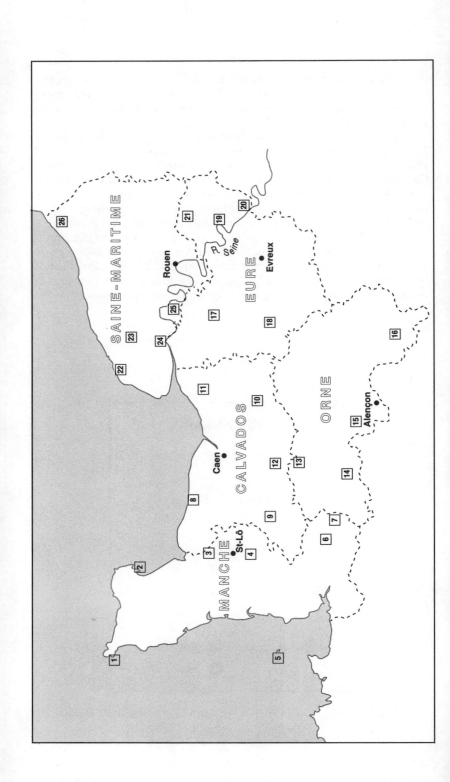

Contents

Orne

Eure

Seine-Maritime

Walking in France

France is almost certainly the best country for walking in Europe. The scenery is widely varied, the tracks are well-maintained and well-waymarked and every Office de Tourisme can offer you an assortment of routes and inexpensive maps of the area.

The excellence of the footpaths of France is due almost entirely to an organisation called the Féderation Française de la Randonnée Pédestre – the FFRP – who over the last half century have waymarked and described routes of all kinds throughout France. Many of the walks in this book are based on their routes, and you will undoubtedly be grateful for some of their waymarking as you follow them. Their long distance paths, the Grandes Randonnées (GR), are the best waymarked paths imaginable, and will invariably lead you past all the most interesting features and best viewpoints in an area. If there is something worth seeing, the Grande Randonnée will take you there. Next there are the Grandes Randonnées du Pays (GRP), circular tours of an area or region which may take, in walking time, anything from a couple of days to a week. They aim to show you the best a region has to offer. And finally there are the Petites Randonnées(PR), the equivalent of our short circular walks, and these are sprinkled generously over the whole country. Each of these route types has its own waymarks, painted on trees, rocks, telegraph poles, or any other convenient surface– the Grandes Randonnées are marked white on red, the Grandes Randonnées du Pays yellow on red and the Petites Randonnées, yellow. You will meet all of them on the walks in this book, so here is all you need to know:

Path continues

Wrong way

Left turn

Right turn

Thus, you are warned of every turn before you reach it, and halted by a cross if you have missed it. Nothing could be simpler! In fairness, it must be said that although Grandes Randonnées are invariably superbly waymarked, the state of a Petite Randonnée may reflect the level of enthusiasm of the local tourist board or walking group. Even so, most are excellent. To accompany these fine routes, the FFRP produces a series of Topoguides, which offer all the relevant information from flora and fauna to history, geology and details of available refreshment. The pity is that only very few have been translated into English, and, oddly, these are generally of the long distance routes. For the rest, at least a working knowledge of French is needed. If you decide to tackle these – or any other described routes – a vocabulary of 'walking words in French' has been included in this book to help out.

Another excellent feature of walking in France is that most paths are open to you – only those marked 'Privé' deny you access. It is accepted that you will not wander on crops or gardens and that you will not leave litter or pick flowers. It should be mentioned that in winter some forest paths are temporarily closed for the period of 'la chasse' – the hunting season – generally from November to February, but these paths will again be marked. In France, farmers and landowners seem much more in tune with walkers than in England and will generally greet you cheerfully. If you can manage just a 'Bonjour' in return it is certain to go down well.

And now the footpaths of France await you – and they are guaranteed to be addictive. Take one short stretch of a Grande Randonnée and you may well be hooked for life! It remains only to wish you 'Bonne route!' – but first, some background to the area:

A little history to set the scene

Early Days

When the Romans arrived in the north of Gaul in the 1st century BC, they found the coast and Seine valley occupied by fierce and warlike tribes of Celtic origin. The remainder of this northern land was covered by forest. The tribes resisted the invasion, but Julius Caesar had his eye on Britain across the water and the land bordering the Channel was important for his ambitions. The Romans remained – and integrated with the local people – for over 500 years. In 486 AD, the Frankish King Clovis defeated these Gallo-Romans at the Battle of Soissons and subsequently annexed all the north of France. Clovis married Clotilde, a Christian, and it was she who encouraged the building of the first abbeys in the Seine valley. A couple of centuries later, Rouen, St. Wandrille and Jumièges stood proudly beside the Seine – and their wealth attracted the interest of the Vikings. In the ninth century, they arrived each summer in their high-prowed boats and worked their way up the Seine in a series of raids that were becoming increasingly terrifying.

The leaders of these Norsemen were always fierce and bloodthirsty, but around 890 there appeared one Rollo, said to be over 7ft tall (too tall to ride a horse!) and quarrelsome to go with it. He had been thrown out of Norway for stealing the king's cattle. Rollo fought his way to power in his new land and was causing so much trouble that the King of France, ungenerously named Charles the Simple, decided to buy him off, make over the northern territories to him and invite him to become the first Duke of Normandy. Rollo accepted, promptly forsook his former ways, and became Christian – but Christianity did not mean monogamy, and he and all his successors kept a handful of concubines and thus had many sons. The great-great-grandson of

Rollo was Robert, a determined character who had wrested the duke-dom from the hands of his brother with the aid of a little poison. Robert lived at Falaise Castle, from the windows of which he one day espied young Arletta, a tanner's daughter, working in the fields beside the river. Arletta bore him two children – the son, not unreasonably, was known as William the Bastard.

William the Conqueror

William was just eight years old when his father died while on a cru-sade. With his life in danger, his mother smuggled him away to the country where he was raised among peasant folk – and emerged as ambitious as his forebears. In his late teens, he began the conquest of more territory in France, and in 1066 turned his sights on England. Edward the Confessor had no issue, the nearest relation in England being Harold, the Earl of Wessex. There is a story that Harold was one day shipwrecked off Normandy and, in gratitude for his rescue, prom-ised William the throne of England after Edward's death. Visit the Bayeux tapestry for more details! This may or may not be so, but the Witan, the ruling body in England, was aware of the problems with the succession. On Edward's demise they rushed to find Harold and had him crowned the same day. When the news came to William, he was said to have fallen silent for many hours. Emerging from his reverie, he announced his plans – an immediate invasion on an unprecedented scale. Seven hundred ships crossed the channel to the Battle of Hastings and Harold was famously shot in the eye. William was crowned King of England on Christmas Day 1066.

Normandy ruled from England – or England ruled from Normandy

William the Conqueror died in 1087, leaving three sons to dispute the duchy of Normandy and the kingdom of England. The youngest son, Henry, triumphed. He himself had two sons, one of whom was set to take over the lands in France, the other the same in England. Both boys were lost in a shipwreck off Barfleur, thus again plunging Nor-mandy – and England – into chaos. Henry's solution was to marry his daughter, Matilda, to Geoffrey of Anjou – a man who habitually wore a sprig of broom (genêt) in his cap! Amid much confusion, their son Henry eventually became Henry II Plantagenet of Normandy and then in 1154, Henry II of England.

The first son of Henry II was Richard the Lionheart. He was away on a crusade when he heard that brother John had teamed up with Philippe-Auguste of France to take over Normandy. He returned home immediately and was doing well in reversing matters when he suddenly contracted gangrene and died. Brother John Lackland took over the reins – this was the John of Magna Carta fame in England. John put up only a poor defence to Philippe-Auguste's incursions and soon was left with only the territory along the Seine – guarded by

Château Gaillard. That itself fell by a cunning invasion through the latrines (see Walk 19) and Philippe-Auguste soon walked into Rouen. In 1204, Normandy was under French rule for the first time.

French Normandy and Joan of Arc

A short spell of peace in Normandy ended with the arrival of Edward III of England on French soil in 1346. The Hundred Years War followed with much fighting on Norman soil, and Henry V's victory at Agincourt in 1415 was one of the most decisive battles. The French throne would have passed to England shortly afterwards, but Henry V unfortunately died at the wrong moment and the war went on. In the midst of all this commotion, the daughter of a farmer in Domrémy claimed she had heard voices telling her that she could oust the English from France. Somehow gaining an audience with the future Charles VII, she persuaded him to give her command of an army. Joan herself donned a suit of white armour and they set out to relieve the siege of Orléans. The deed was accomplished and Joan became a national heroine. Fighting a later battle, she was taken prisoner and put in Rouen Castle, charged with heresy and witchcraft. The trial was held before the Bishop of Beauvais, who had interests along with the English, and Joan was found guilty. Her refusal to recant led to her being burnt at the stake in the market place of Rouen in 1431. The battles continued for almost another 20 years, before the English finally lost their last foothold on French soil.

The Middle Ages and the Revolution

In the 16th century there was more turbulence in Normandy in the shape of the Wars of Religion. The University of Caen and the city of Rouen were strongholds of the Protestant Huguenots under Henry IV. There was much fighting in the region before the Edict of Nantes finally granted the Huguenots freedom of worship. The 16th century was also a time of seafaring discovery, with Norman explorers going out to New World. Quebec was founded by Samuel de Champlain from Dieppe and many Normans subsequently left for Canada. In 1643, Louis XIV, the 'Sun-King' arrived on the throne. His reign was known for its dissolute spending and for its lack of firm rule. Louis was persuaded to revoke the Edict of Nantes, thus supporting the Catholic Church. Backing the return of the exiled catholic James II to England, the French navy was attacked and destroyed by an Anglo-Dutch fleet at the Battle of la Hougue. The military architect Vauban was subsequently called in to defend the port – and the towers and fort he built can still be seen at St. Vaast-la-Hougue. Unreasonable taxation imposed by Louis and his successors led to the 'Barefoot Revolt' in Normandy – and subsequently to the Revolution.

Normandy played little part in the Revolution, but still managed to support two anti-revolutionary groups in the following Reign of Terror. The first was the Girondins, the original ruling party after the

Revolution who were succeeded by the notorious Jacobins. They later found a stronghold in Caen. It was in defence of this group that Charlotte Corday left her home in Caen to seek the 'People's Friend' Marat in Paris, and gained fame for all time by daring to stab him in his bath. She lost her head for the act. The second anti-revolutionary group was the Chouans, named from their secret call, imitating that of the screech owl. Their subversive activities continued until Napoleon brought a measure of peace to France at the beginning of the 19th century

The Belle Époque.

Until the 19th century, bathing in the sea was not considered a pleasurable activity – rather it was reserved for the cure of skin complaints, and in particular, scabies. The Duchess of Berry changed all that in 1834 by daring to dip her toes in the sea at Deauville – and actually changing on the beach for the adventure. Others soon followed her example, and the towns of Normandy's north coast became the summer playgrounds of the rich and aristocratic from Paris. They were joined by the talented and artistic – Monet and his impressionist colleagues, the writers Maupassant, Flaubert and Dumas. Étretat was a particular favourite with them all.

War – and the Battle of Normandy

Normandy saw no fighting in the First World War – the front line remained well to the east, but the supplies for the troops arrived through her channel ports. The Second World War was a very different matter. After the failed raid by the Canadians on Dieppe in the summer of 1942, it was realised that an allied invasion must be carefully planned, with back-up of provisions and ammunition for the troops. Since it would take some time to capture a port, they must make arrangements to take their own. Two 'floating harbours' were to be towed across the Channel – as it happened, only the British one, sited at Arromanches, was to survive – and the beaches on either side were to be the landing beaches, code-named Utah, Omaha, Gold, Juno and Sword.

The 6th June 1944 was a day of tremendous heroism. Those who lost their lives are buried in the cemeteries along the coast, and there are other relics of this initial battle – the battery at Longues, the bunkers at the Pointe du Hoc, the memorial at Colleville and more. The allied troops took longer than was expected to gain ground across Normandy, and fighting was bitter. The traditional 'bocage' of high banks and sunken tracks impeded progress and combat became hand-to-hand. St. Lô and Caen had to be totally destroyed before they could be captured. Mortain was the scene of the last German offensive – an attempt to cut off the American forces from the source of their supplies. The town was laid to ruin, but the attack was repelled. The bravery of the defending American troops is now chronicled for all to read on a peaceful wooded hill above Mortain. This 'coun-ter-attack' by the Germans turned out to be a military blunder. The entire retreating 7th army was trapped by the encircling allies in the Falaise pocket, thus rapidly bringing to an end the Battle of Normandy on 21st of August. To commemorate its 50th anniversary, eight themed itineraries were devised, following the course of the battle across the province. Every scene of note now bears a post telling its story – Nor-mandy can never forget.

Recovery was hard, but the towns were rebuilt. Ancient buildings were sympathetically restored, but Normandy did not throw away the opportunity to modernise itself. The old ways of life have changed since the war. Agriculture is still the main industry, but it is less impor-tant than in pre-war times. Fishing too is in decline. Tourism has become important to Normandy, and 'green' tourism in particular is encouraged. The country has a wealth of eco-museums and other exhibition centres of high quality. Every Tourist Office is teeming with literature of all kinds and they are very keen to promote walking as an eco-friendly form of recreation. There is no doubt Normandy would warmly welcome an invasion of British walkers on its many well-marked trails.

Dictionary of Walking Words

anse	a cove, a small bay
atteindre	to reach
balisage	waymarking
bifurquer	to fork
Blanc (blanche)	white
bleu(e)	blue
bois	a wood
bosquet	a spinney, a copse
chemin	a way, a path
colline	a hill
contourner	to go around, to skirt
creux	sunken or hollowed out
dessous	under
dessus	above
droit (tout droit)	straight ahead
droite	right
église	church
empierré	stony or metalled (as in road)
emprunter	to take (as in direction)
étang	a pond, a pool
en face	opposite
fourche	a fork
franchir	to clear, to cross
gauche	left
goudronnée	tarmacked
grimper	to climb
hameau	hamlet
jaune	yellow
jusqu'à	as far as
longer	to skirt
mener	to lead
monter	to climb
niveau	a level
patte d'oie	multiple path or road junction
pente	slope
prairie	a meadow
rouge	red
route	a road, track or direction
ruisseau	a stream
sentier	a footpath, a track
sous-bois	undergrowth
suivre	to follow
talus	a slope or bank
tourner	to turn
traverser	to cross
variante	alternative route
vert(e)	green
virer	to bend or turn

Offices de Tourisme

Walk	Location	Address
1	Beaumont-Hague	Office de Tourisme de la Hague, BP 119, 50440 BEAUMONT-HAGUE
2	St. Vaast-la-Hougue	Place Général de Gaulle, 50550 ST.VAAST-LA-HOUGUE
3	Carentan	Boulevard de Verdun – BP 229, 50500 CARENTAN
4	St. Lô	Place Général de Gaulle, 50000 ST. LÔ
5	Granville	4, Cours Jonville, 50400 GRANVILLE
6	Mortain	Rue du Bourglopin, 50140 MORTAIN
7	Domfront	Rue St.-Julien – BP 7. 61700 DOMFRONT
8	Arromanches	2, Rue de Maréchal Joffre, 14117 ARROMANCHES-LES-BAINS
9	Vire	Square de la Résistance, 14500 VIRE
10	Livarot	1, Place G. Bisson, 14140 LIVAROT
11	Pont-l'Evêque	Rue St. Michel – BP 77, 14130 PONT-L'EVÊQUE
12	Clécy	Place de la Mairie, 14570 CLÉCY
13	Putanges-Pont-Écrepin	Place de la Mairie, 61210 PUTANGES-PONT-ÉCREPIN
14	Bagnoles-de-l'Orne	Place du Marché – BP 32, 61140 BAGNOLES-DE-L'ORNE
15	Carrouges	Parc Naturel Régional Normandie-Maine, Maison du Parc, 61320 CARROUGES
16	Bellême	Bd. Bansard des Bois, 61130 BELLÊME
17	Brionne	Place de l'Église, 27800 BRIONNE
18	Conches-en-Ouche	Rue Aristide Briand – BP 15, 27190 CONCHES-EN-OUCHE
19	Les Andelys	1, rue Philippe-Auguste – BP 242, 27702 LES-ANDELYS
20	Vernon	36, Rue Carnot – BP 110, 27201 VERNON
21	Lyons-la-Forêt	20, Rue de l'Hôtel de Ville, 27480 LYONS-LA-FORÊT
22	Étretat	Place Maurice Guillard – BP 3, 76790 ÉTRETAT
23	Cany-Barville	Place Robert Gabel, 76450 CANY-BARVILLE
24	Caudebec-en-Caux	Place du Général de Gaulle, 76490 CAUDEBEC-EN-CAUX
25	Duclair	Mairie, 76480 DUCLAIR
26	Criel-su-Mer	Mairie, 76910 CRIEL-SUR-MER

Recommended Publications

Michelin Tourist Guide to Normandy ISBN 2-06-134802-5

Insight Guides – Normandy ISBN 962-421-202-3

Berlitz Travel Guide – Normandy ISBN 2-8315-0232-2

The Rough Guide – Brittany and Normandy, Greg Ward ISBN 1-85828-019-2

And, in French only:

Découvrir la Normandie en marchant, Dominique Le Brun (Éditions Franck Mercier) ISBN 2-86868-141-7

Normandy on the Internet

There are plenty of websites relating to Normandy. Here are just a few you might find useful.

www.ffrp.asso.fr

This is the website of the French rambling association, the Fédération Française de la Randonnée Pédestre (FFRP). Along with other information (in French), the site lists and describes the major Topoguides and gives information on ordering direct – a cheaper option than buying in England.

www.brittany-ferries.com

The website of Brittany Ferries, giving sailing schedules, prices, online reservations and details of holiday properties all over Normandy (and elsewhere).

www.poef.com/poef

The website of P and O European Ferries, with sailings from Portsmouth to Cherbourg and Le Havre. Gives schedules, prices and opportunity for reservations.

www.posl.com

The website of P and O Stena Line – an independent company offering half-hourly super-ferries between Dover and Calais. Prices and reservations.

www.eurotunnel.co.uk

Eurotunnel is probably the preferred mode of travel if you are taking your pets with you (they might enjoy a walking holiday!) This site gives schedules, prices and online booking. There are also details about the Pets Travel Scheme, telling you exactly what you need and what will happen on the day – and spelling out the price of Rover's ticket.

Several other companies are operating cross-channel ferries – check with any Travel Agent.

www.normandy-tourism.org

This is the official tourist site, and it offers you just about anything you want to know – main attractions, photographs, history, accommodation, maps, D-Day sites, sport, churches and plenty more.

http://gofrance.miningco.com/travel/gofrance/library/weekly/aa020899.htm

This site is entitled The D-Day Links and gives 'a relatively complete collection of what can currently be found on the Net pertaining to D-Day and the Battle of Normandy'.

La Petite Cascade, Mortain (Walk 6)

Manche

1. Coastal paths around the Nez de Jobourg

The Nez de Jobourg is a bare rocky promontory jutting into the western sea. To the north is the lovely sweeping Baie d'Ecalgrain, to the south, the granite slopes of the highest cliffs in Europe. Here are two walks that can easily be rolled into one along the wildest coastline in Normandy.

Grade: Moderate, but strenuous along cliffs.

Distance: Cliff circuit 7.5km (4¾ miles); Bay circuit 8km (5 miles). This can be reduced to 5km by starting from the car park beside the bay – but do go up to the Nez for the view; combined route, 10km (6¼ miles)

Time: Cliff circuit 3 hours; Bay circuit 2½ hours; Combined circuit 4 hours

Map: IGN Série Bleue 1110 E.

Start and finish: Parking for the Nez de Jobourg. The bay circuit could be started from the car park at the Baie d'Ecalgrain.

How to get there: From Beaumont-Hague continue north on the D901. After passing the Nuclear Power Station, turn left where signed to the Nez de Jobourg. There is parking on the right just before the end of the road.

Refreshment: Beside the car park is a little hut, the Buvette des Grottes, selling drinks and snacks in summer time. Overlooking the Nez de Jobourg and just along from the car park is the Auberge des Grottes – which again may be closed in winter. Opposite the church in Jobourg is the pleasant Restaurant de la Bruyère.

Notes: In the best of weathers, it would be reasonable to undertake either of these circuits wearing trainers. Walking boots are advised out of season. The cliff path is not only narrow, but very exposed and should not be attempted in high winds. It cannot be considered suitable for young children at any time. You should carry fluid in warm weather – there is no refreshment en route – and protection from the sun would be advisable. The views are excellent, so bring your binoculars. And if you bring your bathing costume as well, you can enjoy a swim in the Baie d'Ecalgrain at the end of the day. And for good measure, the bay faces west and you nay be lucky enough to witness a spectacular sunset.

Waymarking: The circuit of the cliffs is waymarked in yellow, and that of the bay in blue throughout.

Introduction

To the west of Cherbourg a long finger of land points out into the English Channel, at its tip the Cap de la Hague. This is wild country, its coastline bare granite cliffs backed by moorland. It is also incredibly beautiful. Here you will find none of the trappings of the popular seaside – no fun fairs, boat trips or candy floss stalls. The few who holiday

Anse de Pivette, seen from the GR223

here come to find nature in the raw, and in places it is quite
awe-inspiring.

It is something of a shock in this remote country to come across the
Nuclear Power Station at Beaumont-Hague. The blow is a little softened by the delicate pastel shades in which the buildings are painted.
Be reassured – it intrudes little on your walk. Once you turn out
towards the Nez de Jobourg, you will find nothing more to intrude on
the natural scene than the little Auberge des Grottes beyond the car
park. It is certainly an Auberge with a view – a view that is improved if
you walk out just a few paces towards the headland, which is in fact
the Nez de Voidries. From here you can look south across a little bay
of boulders and shingle to the barren Nez de Jobourg or north along a
long curving sandy beach fringed with gorse and heather. These
opposing views offer you two walks through different terrain – or,
better still, a long walk of contrasts.

The northern walk along the Baie d'Ecalgrain is by far the gentler.
The path descends giving you good views of the sea and the island of
Alderney offshore. After skirting the beach, you climb to a track running along the heights behind the bay, and here the views are even
more spectacular, on a clear day extending to Guernsey. Returning
through villages and farmland, a track with yet more good views brings
you back to the edge of the bay.

If you have chosen the cliff walk, you will head out towards the
very different coast in the south. Before you go, just a word of caution:
this walk is not for the young, the old or the faint-hearted – but it is a
walk to remember! The cliffs here are more than 120 metres high but
they are not sheer. Instead, the folds of gorse-clad granite slope very

steeply to the foaming turquoise sea below and along them winds the path, a narrow twisting ribbon, crossing outcrops and dipping into the valleys between. This path is a Grande Randonnée and well-waymarked, but you will certainly need a head for heights. If you have it – go! It is truly very beautiful and the wild flowers beside your path are an added bonus. If you have the time and the inclination, these two walks are very easily joined, and the combination makes an excellent introduction to this splendidly untamed and unspoilt corner of Normandy.

The Walk

1. From the car park, continue along the road to the bar/restaurant. This is the Auberge des Grottes, so called because there are three caves – virtually inaccessible -at the foot of these high cliffs. Passing the building, immediately turn right on the broad grassy track, which bears the white on red waymarks of the Grande Randonnée. There are fine views of the Baie d'Ecalgrain ahead and beyond it, the lighthouse out to sea on rocks near the Cap de la Hague. The path gradually descends and eventually reaches a wooded valley rich in wild flowers. Soon a stream joins you from the right and, lower down, the path crosses it on stepping stones. The path leads on to a wide gravelled track, which begins to climb. As the track levels out again, you reach a junction with another track that doubles back uphill to the right.

2. This is the parting of the ways – for the cliff circuit turn right here, for the bay or the combined route, continue ahead.

For the cliff circuit only

Turn right at this junction and continue on the broad track uphill. You have now left the Grande Randonnée and there are occasional yellow or blue waymarks. The track climbs very steeply and after 15 minutes or so you reach a T- junction at which you turn right. The path now begins a slower descent. After a sharp left-hand corner, at which you ignore a track going ahead and continue on the road, there is a very steep descent into the village where you meet the road at point 6 on the map and·turn right.

For the bay or combined circuits

Continue ahead on the Grande Randonnée at this junction. If the day is reasonable, you should be able to see the island of Alderney out to sea. After a short while you come in sight of a car parking area beside the bay and the Grande Randonnée goes through a gate on the left and crosses a small field to reach it.

3. Leave the car park continuing north. Just before you reach the road, a path leaves on the left and follows beside it. This path shortly joins the road again, but at this point, the Grande

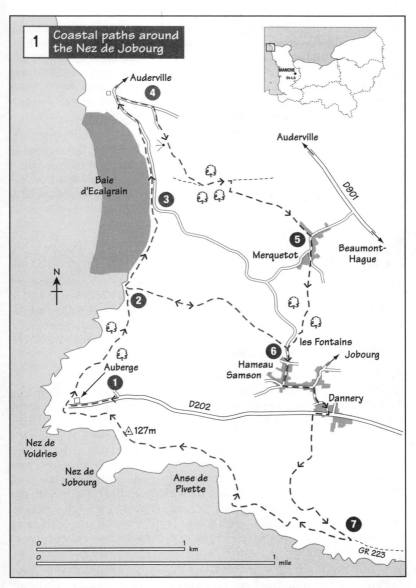

1 Coastal paths around the Nez de Jobourg

Randonnée bears left and takes a route well below the level of the road. Following it, you eventually reach the road again much higher up the hill. Now turn left and continue up the hill on the road, ignoring the GR, which takes itself off on the left again. At the top of the hill, just before reaching the house, take the first road on the right. After a further 5 minutes walking, you come to a fork.

4. At this fork, take the right hand option which becomes a track. This track continues ahead with most glorious views over the bay. After a short time, a blue waymarked track joins from the right and the track you are on bears sharply left and becomes sunken and much narrower. On reaching a clearing area, your route bears right on to a waymarked track. Continuing on this track for per-haps 15 minutes you reach the village of Merquetot.

5. Reaching the road at a corner, turn right and continue to the fork. Now bear left, uphill, and where the road corners left, continue on the blue waymarked track that proceeds straight ahead. This is now a pleasant high-banked track with views. After a few minutes it begins to descend and reaches the road beside a water-spout at a place called les Fontaines. Turn left on this road and walk uphill to a junction where a road comes in on the right.

6. This is a junction where more choices must be made.

For the bay circuit

Turn right here, and continue uphill on the road. At a sharp right hand corner, ignore a grassy track coming in on the left. Continue ahead to a track junction where you turn left on a wide stony track following the yellow and blue waymarks. This track goes downhill quite steeply, with good views of the bay ahead. Soon you arrive at Point 2 and can turn left to return to the starting point.

For the cliff and combined circuits

Continue on the road into the pretty stone village of Hameau Samson. At the first cross-roads keep straight ahead, but at the T-junction at the top of the village turn left. At the next junction, turn right and con-tinue through the stone farms of the hamlet of Dannery to reach the main road to the Nez. Turn right here, and then, just after the last houses of the hamlet, turn left on a broad track. This soon becomes tarmacked, and then becomes stony again. The path descends until the sea itself comes into view and then clings to the hillside with the sea below on the right. Shortly you reach a post at a track junction. The views here are quite spectacular, with the cliff ahead blazing yellow with gorse in season and beyond it, the wide sweeping curve of the Bay of Vauville.

7. Here double back to the right (sea now on the left) and join the Grande Randonnée, curving downhill into the gorse above the rocky shores. Soon enough the path begins climbing again. No words are necessary to direct you from here – the path is quite clear, and as a GR is well waymarked with white on red flashes, but you will certainly need to take care. The sea thunders away below you as you round one headland after another on this path amid gorse and flowers. The terrain becomes more barren as you approach the Nez de Jobourg, which appears as a dark hump of

rock jutting far into the sea. A tiny path leads out to it – don't worry, it's not for you. The Nez itself is an ornithological reserve and so gets the occasional brave visitor. A further sweeping descent and hard climb now return you to the welcoming Auberge on the cliff top from which the journey began.

More Walks in the Area

The Office de Tourisme of the district of la Hague has produced a truly excellent and comprehensive set of walking leaflets (approx. 20). Between them, they cover almost all the coastline and much inland as well and it seems that every commune has produced at least one walk. The maps are easy to read, there is very little text and the waymarking on the ground is good. Among so many good walks, it is difficult to pick out a few, but consider the routes around Vauville. The village itself is most attractive and between village and sea is an inland lake that is an ornithological reserve. Behind it, on the high ground, is a very exciting viewpoint at the Belvédère du Thot, while just up the road is the Pierre Pouquelée, a somewhat ruined allée couverte (gallery grave). Just south of Vauville is Biville, famous for its enormous dunes (also a nature reserve) and for the view from the Calvary above them.

On the west coast above the Baie d'Ecalgrain there are some fine walks starting from Auderville. From here, you can walk down to the little port of Goury with its lifeboat, the only safe haven on the treacherous Alderney Race. Out to sea is the lighthouse on its rock, and to the north, the cape itself.

The north coast of la Hague is similarly impressive. The rocks of Castel Vendon make a superb viewpoint over the entrance to Cherbourg harbour and the port of Omonville-la-Rogue – take the 8km circuit from Gréville-Hague.

All these circular walks are contained in the folder entitled Découverte de la Hague à Pied, which can be obtained from the very helpful Office de Tourisme at Beaumont-Hague.

If you want to make sure of covering every inch of this magnificent coastline, you will have to take to the GR 223, which follows it all the way. This may not be easy, as it is not really served by public transport. If you have two cars or a friend to pick you up there is no problem, but otherwise the Office de Tourisme at Beaumont may be able to help you find a taxi. It is easy to follow a Grande Randonnée with just an IGN map, but if you want to do it in style, the Topoguide Tour du Cotentin (Ref. 200) will give you maps and tell you all you need to know about the coastal path all the way around the peninsula. Refreshments, bus and train connections and overnight stopping places are included – but again, some knowledge of French would be helpful.

Places of interest nearby

There are two interesting châteaux in the region and each has fine gardens worth visiting. The gardens of the handsome 16th century Château de Nacqueville (close to Urville-Nacqueville) are known for their rhododendron display in late spring. A visit to the Château de Vauville would combine well with the already mentioned walk in the area. The proximity of the Gulf Stream gives this region a mild climate, and the gardens of this château exhibit sub-tropical vegetation with many palm trees.

Near Gréville-Hague is the village of Gruchy, which was the birthplace of Jean-François Millet, the impressionist. Tourism has recently arrived here, and his house has now been turned into a museum. From Gruchy, it is just a short walk to the coastal viewpoint of Castel Vendon – see the More Walks section.

And for something very different, it is possible to visit that Nuclear Power Station. 75% of the electricity of France is produced in this way and the French are keen to convince everyone of the benefits. Farther down the coast (and clearly in view on the Vauville walk) is the nuclear power station at Flamanville, and this is even more geared up to visitors, as it offers an information centre, exhibition, question time and guided tours.

2. St. Vaast-la-Hougue and the Val de Saire

This is a walk of contrasts. The bustling fishing port of St. Vaast-la-Hougue and its well-guarded bay are the gateway to a steep green valley of typical Normandy bocage – stone farmhouses, high-banked tracks and masses of wild-flowers.

Grade: Easy

Distance: 13km (8 miles) – a short cut is available, reducing the distance by about 3km., but it does cut out the best part of the bocage.

Time: 3½ hours

Map: IGN Série Bleue 1310 O

Start and finish: Chapelle des Marins (Chapel of the Mariners), St. Vaast-la-Hougue

How to get there: The chapel is on the sea front, immediately south of the port

Refreshment: You should try the oysters – there are seafood restaurants all along the front! But there are also many opportunities for more conventional eating in St. Vaast.

Notes: This is a fairly easy walk on good tracks and in summer should not require stouter footwear than trainers. It would be advisable to carry water as there is no refreshment en route. Although the inland lanes are well-shaded, the walk ends with open country behind the coast and a long stretch along the exposed sea-wall – some protection from the sun may be appreciated on a hot day. You may like to take binoculars for the coastal views, and a bathing costume for a swim at the end of the day.

Waymarking: The route – and short cut – are waymarked in yellow throughout. The first part of the walk is on a Grande Randonnée, the GR 223

Introduction

In May of 1692, the seas off St. Vaast-la-Hougue were the scene of an historic encounter. The French fleet was on its way to invade England, its aim the restoration to the throne of the Catholic James II, who had been deposed by William of Orange. The combined English and Dutch fleets arrived in greater numbers, battle was engaged, and soon many of the damaged French ships were forced to take shelter in the harbour of la Hougue – where the English were less than chivalrous and promptly set fire to them all. Louis XIV decided to defend la Hougue against similar occurrences by installing twin forts on the islands of Tatihou and la Hougue. They were built by that ubiquitous military architect Vauban, and each was equipped with a tower and canons – which, in fact, have never been used. Both forts are still there today.

St Vaast-la-Hougue is no longer a naval base, but rather a fishing port. On the main road beside the harbour, rough piles of dripping nets lie across the carriageway – the traffic threads its way between. Deep-tanned fishermen busy themselves with their livelihood, while opposite those on more leisurely pursuits browse among the menus of the seafood restaurants – or opt for a 'do-it-yourself' with a visit to the fish market at the end of the row. St. Vaast (pronounced 'Va') is a fascinating place. Beyond the harbour home of the fishing fleet is a pleasure port, and then a long shallow bay devoted to *ostreiculture*. This is the oyster capital of the north, and when the tide falls a motley procession of tractors can be seen heading out to tend the black rows of beds filling the bay.

Across the bay is the island of Tatihou – you can go out to it by boat from the harbour or chance your luck on foot at low tide on a passage through the oyster beds known as the Run. Apparently the latter is possible when the tidal coefficient is greater than 70 – it can be checked at the harbour. The fort on Tatihou now houses a restaurant and bookshop, and there is also a Maritime Museum, with relics from ships sunk in the Battle of la Hougue. A nature reserve offers opportunities for bird-watching. The smaller island of la Hougue is connected to the town by a causeway from the south end of the harbour, where you will also find the Chapelle des Marins on its rock projecting into the bay.

The walk starts at this chapel and heads along the bay before turning inland to the countryside of the Val de Saire. Although you may have seen signs to this valley when leaving the boat at Cherbourg, it is probably somewhere to which you have never given a thought. If so,

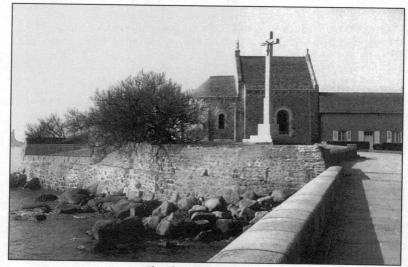

The Chapel of the Mariners

you have been missing something! The Val de Saire is a triangle of Normandy bocage, green countryside of fields, lanes, farms and woodland, attractive enough to warrant its epithet 'the garden beside the sea'. This is particularly true in springtime, which here sees bank after bank bursting with colour – celandines, wood anemones, violets, daffodils and above all, primroses. Normandy is a land rich in wild flowers, but nowhere can they be more stunning than in the Val de Saire early in the year. When you emerge from the flower-banked tracks, there are fine views of the distant bay before the return. The route comes out beside Réville bay with its oyster beds and you can enjoy a long bracing walk home along the sea-wall and past the fishing fleet at the port.

The Walk

1. Leaving the Chapelle des Marins, walk away from the port and take a track behind the old anchor which leads on to the sea wall. Following the GR waymarks (white on red), turn down some steps and then left behind a house. Continue on the path and road behind the sea wall. Just before reaching the causeway, turn right on to a grassy track beside the bay. At the end of this grassy area, turn right on a track beside the hedge and then left along the road – still following the waymarks of the Grande Randonnée. Keep ahead on this road (i.e. left at the fork) and eventually you are lead back to the sea again.

2. Soon a corner is reached at which you are informed that you may only take the path on the left at low tide. At other times, you must turn through the wooden barrier and keep ahead on the waymarked track. The GR waymarks now lead you through an area of new building and then left to the sea again. Passing an oyster farm, you are invited to call in for a taste! The track now continues beside the sea and soon joins a road, passing another oyster farm. Where this road turns away from the sea, continue ahead. Soon the path crosses a stream, and then bears right around the grounds of a house. On reaching the track, turn right – still following both Grande Randonnée and yellow flashes. After 5 minutes or so, you reach the main road.

3. Cross the road diagonally to the right, joining the rue de Vieux Puits. After 150 metres, at the cross-roads with the lavoir (ancient village washing place) opposite, turn right. At the sharp bend in the road, ignore the track going off on the left, but 50 metres or so farther on, turn left on the Chemin des Noyers. Climb to the main road and cross it to reach the church at Quettehou.

4. The church overlooks the bay with its islands – you are invited to go into the cemetery to get the best view! The short cut leaves the route beside the church – it will be described at the end of the main walk.

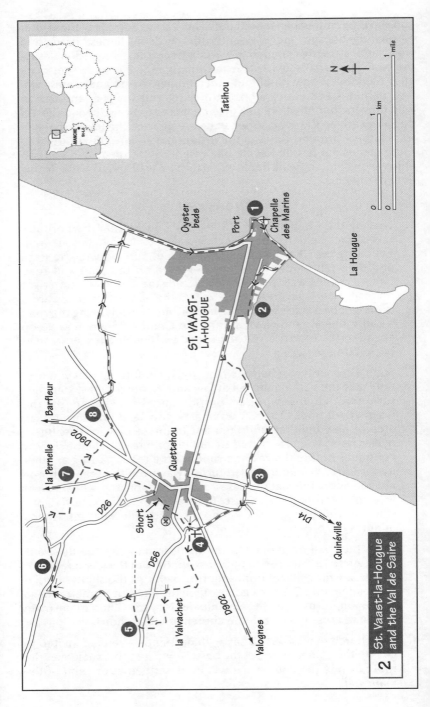

Tatihou

Oyster beds

Port

Chapelle des Marins

La Hougue

ST. VAAST-LA-HOUGUE

Quettehou

Barfleur

la Pernelle

D902

D26

Short cut

Valognes

D902

D56

la Valvachet

D14

Quinéville

2 St. Vaast-la-Hougue and the Val de Saire

22

To continue with the main walk, bear left along the back of the church and take the high-banked track at the end (waymarked in yellow). This attractive path skirts a valley on the right and here you will meet the first of several boards giving information on the vegetation of the bocage. The route bears right at the bottom of the hill and then climbs past some lovely stone farm buildings in the hamlet of le Valvachet. At the junction, turn left on a flower-banked track that climbs gently and reaching the fork at the top of the climb, bear right. Just before reaching the road, a gap in the hedge gives a magnificent view of the bay.

5.   Cross the road to a track opposite, which bears to the right. Where this track reaches the road, the track opposite is waymarked in yellow – ignore it. (could this be for mountain-bikes?). Instead, turn left on the narrow road and follow it through a picturesque valley where an old stone farmhouse overlooks a stream. Climbing again, you enjoy more fine views, and pass a house with a beautiful garden, before reaching a track on the right about 30 metres before the main road. This track itself leads to the main road, and you follow this to the right for about 150 metres (take care!)

6.   Now turn left down yet another sunken track and carry on to meet a road at a sharp corner. Continuing ahead, you soon arrive at a road junction where just about every pole seems to bear a coloured flash. Turn right here on a broad grassy track, and then turn left at a T-junction without any waymarking at all. This high-banked track descends to a road, where again waymarking is curiously absent. Cross straight over on to a rough stony track, which soon reaches a track junction.

7.   Here the short cut joins you from the right (see below). Following the main route, you turn left down a rough steep-sided track, which leads you down to the main road. Cross straight over this to a grassy track opposite (no waymarks again). This track soon brings you to another lesser road where you turn left. Continue approx. 200 metres to the cross-roads.

8.   Turn right here to take the shortest route to the sea (the yellow-flashed route, now meanders, somewhat pointlessly, to the north) The road soon corners left and in about 500 metres reaches a T-junction. Here turn left, follow the road as it corners right, and continue for a further 500 metres to another T-junction. Again turn left and, in 20 metres, you come to a road junction. Turn right on the Route de Dureçu and follow it past the château to a T-junction beside a ruined tower. Turn left and walk ahead to climb the sea wall. The island of Tatihou lies across the bay – at low tide you can see the oyster beds and between them the passage to the island. It's a fine view to enjoy all the way back to the harbour at St. Vaast.

Short Cut

This can also be used to complete a short circular walk from Quettehou missing out the coastal section. You can park at the church – or in the square, joining the route at Point X.

4. With the church on the left, take the second track on the right (waymarked) and descend on this track for about 150 metres to meet the main road (Point X). Cross straight over and follow this waymarked track to another 'main road' at which you turn right and immediately left along the side of a house. At the next main road, cross straight over to the D125 to la Pernelle. As this road bends left, take the waymarked track on the right, which brings you to Point 7

More Walks in the Area

A collection of walks entitled *Découverte du Val de Saire* can be obtained from the Office de Tourisme at St. Vaast (beside the harbour). Here are 18 walks and 3 bike rides – among them many attractive options, including the wild coast and moorland to the north and the inland woods and valley of the River Saire itself. It is difficult to imagine that this area was quite industrialised in the 19th century –a total of 37 water-mills were powered by this river. The walk around le Vast to the west of Quettehou, while passing through most attractive countryside, also shows you something of the industrial past with a waterfall on the site of an old cotton mill and various old houses of the workforce in the town and beside the river. The town also has various gastronomic possibilities that can be investigated – cider, ham omelettes and a special brioche produced at the bakery. The GR du Pays, Val de Saire, passes through the town.

This collection of walks also includes a circuit passing the Phare de Gatteville on the north-east coast . This rather austere lighthouse makes an interesting visit – see below. The Office de Tourisme at Barfleur also has a free leaflet of a circular walk visiting the lighthouse – but you would need a fair command of French as the sketch map here is not of great use and the route is not waymarked. A simpler option would be to follow the GR along the coast from Barfleur to the lighthouse and return by the same route.

If you enjoy long coastal walks, you are well-served at St. Vaast, as the Grande Randonnée can easily be followed to both the north and the south. The distance to Barfleur in the north is about 15km and that to Quinéville in the south (where the GR leaves the coast) about 13km Both these towns have much of interest (see below) and both have a bus service to St. Vaast – ask at the Office de Tourisme for details. If you would like a map of the route and lots more information, get hold of the Topoguide *Tour du Cotentin (Ref. 200)*

Places of interest nearby

The village of la Pernelle, just north of St. Vaast, boasts the very best view of this attractive coastline – a panorama which extends from the lighthouse in the north across Réville bay and Tatihou to the bay of Morsalines and the Marcouf Islands in the south (and on a good day to the northern cliffs of Calvados as well). Follow the signs to the panorama – where there is also an orientation table.

The *Phare de Gatteville* (lighthouse) just north of Barfleur is well worth a visit. A formidable 75 metres in height, it is the second tallest lighthouse in France, and was obviously designed by someone with a mathematical bent as it has 7 floors, 52 windows and 365 steps. The view from the top is spectacular! The lighthouse is open all day, every day in summer – but note that, in true French tradition, it takes a long lunch break.

The little town of Barfleur has an attractive harbour where you can stroll beside the fishing fleet along a quay strewn with nets and lobster pots, and perhaps sample some of the mussels for which it is famous. It is an easy walk from here along the coastal path (the GR) to the Phare de Gatteville – just follow the white on red waymarks from the end of the harbour.

South of St. Vaast at Quinéville is the *Musée de la Liberté* – a rather different museum in that there are no weapons of warfare to be seen. Instead, the museum confines itself to details of French life under the occupation with a variety of displays. It is open daily in summer.

3. The marshlands of Cotentin

The *marais* – the vast central marsh of Cotentin – is now a regional park where wildfowl abound and storks are summer visitors. This walk will give you a good chance of spotting some as you amble beside the River Vire before returning on higher ground.

Grade: Easy

Distance: 10.5km (6½ miles)

Time: 3 hours

Map: IGN Série Bleue 1312 E

Start and finish: The bridge at St. Fromond

How to get there: From Carentan, take the N174 heading south. 1km south of St. Jean-de-Daye, turn east on the D8 to St. Fromond (2km.)

Refreshment: There are two bar/restaurants and a hotel in St. Fromond, but nothing else en route. Picnic tables are provided beside the Canal de Vire et Taute at la Rivière.

Notes: This is a very easy walk with only one or two gradients. Much of the route is on quiet roads where you will be quite happy in trainers, but there is a section on the river bank where the long grass can soak your feet after wet weather. You should on no account venture on to the *marais* even if it looks dry – you can't tell what is underneath! There is little shade on this walk – on a hot day you may need protection from the sun and you should carry a supply of water. Binoculars are useful for viewing the birds.

Waymarking: The route is waymarked in blue throughout.

Introduction

Stretching in a wide band across the heart of Cotentin is the *marais*, low-lying country crossed by a network of rivers and canals draining to the sea on either side. In between them is a swamp of reed and sedge and willow, a land of wide skies and distant horizons. There is a unique flavour to this environment and since 1991 the area has been given the status of a regional park – the *Parc Naturel Régional des Marais du Cotentin et du Bessin*. It is a park that reaches from the haven of St. Germain-sur-Ay in the west to the Baie des Veys in the east and farther on behind the *débarquement* beaches of Calvados

What you see in the marais will depend on the season. In summer there may be flat grassland as far as the eye can see, broken only by the odd clump of small trees and the raised banks of canalised rivers. In winter and spring, or after heavy rains, the marais may be *blanchi* – white with water. It is said that if the sea level rose by just 10 metres, the north of Cotentin would be an island. The few villages on the marais are not surprisingly confined to areas of higher ground, and in many of them you can still see the old *maisons torchis*, traditional

The bridge over the River Vire at St. Fromond

buildings of red clay and straw. Sadly, the traditional flat-bottomed boats – *gabarres* – no longer ply the waterways with their cargoes of fertiliser and building materials from the quarries – but you can still see one in its shelter in the village square at Tribehou.

The watery nature of the marais makes it an ornithological paradise. Being on the migration route from Scandinavia to Africa, many species of wildfowl come and go with the seasons. Most spectacular of all in recent years are the storks, who are summer visitors – look out for their large white forms wheeling in the air or standing silently beside the marsh. In summer time, the butterflies are also spectacular and rare wild flowers thrive on the marshland. Details of all there is to see can be found at the Park Headquarters, the Manoir de Cantepie, which in itself is more than worth a visit.

Being a regional park, there are many walks described in the area. Unfortunately, they are largely on tarmac as there are few safe paths on the marshes. The route of this walk takes you out to the marais along the raised banks of the River Vire and then along the canal joining the Vire and the Taute. This latter was constructed under Napoleon with the intention of minimising the frequent flooding of the area. From its banks, you may have an opportunity to spot some storks. Farther along the route climbs above the marshland on higher ground with good views. It returns to St. Fromond past the lonely grey *Abbatiale* church and its farm, their origins dating back to the 11th century.

The Walk

1. From the bridge at St. Fromond, head north on the towpath (river on your right). After a few minutes walking, you reach the point at which the canal leaves the River Vire. Continue ahead here, now on the towpath of the canal. This shortly crosses a bridge over the canal to gain the opposite bank. At the next bridge, you have a fine view across the marais to the north-east, and this is a good place to scan the horizon for storks. Continue to keep your eyes open as you walk to the next bridge at la Rivière.

2. The ruins of the Château de la Rivière lie in the field on the right of the canal. Now cross this bridge beside the picnic site and continue on the road for about 300 metres. Turn right following the blue waymarks. The rough track you are on bends right, left and right again and then passes brick quarries to reach the road.

3. At the road, turn left, still keeping along the edge of the quarry. The road climbs and descends again to the cross-roads at la Briquerie. Here cross straight over and after about 400 metres, turn right on a blue waymarked track leading into the wood. A notice tells you that this is private property and that only walkers are allowed. A pleasant uphill path through the woodland now follows, and you emerge in a high field with good views back over the marais. Leave the field through a gate and continue following the blue waymarks to reach the main road.

4. Turn left on the road and in about 150 yards, take the road on the right. This leads on into an attractive steep-sided track with views of the *Abbatiale* (abbey church) ahead. At the bottom of the hill, the track crosses the stream and climbs again to reach another road. Here turn left and keep to the road for just 100 metres, to where a blue-waymarked track leads off on the right. (Keeping ahead on this road, followed by a left at the road junction would be a short cut to the Abbatiale)

5. Turn right on to this track, which soon descends between high banks. On reaching the road at the bottom, turn right and climb to the village of la Liberderie. Where the road corners to the right, keep straight ahead on the track running beside the farm. From this track, there are good views across the sloping fields to the Abbatiale. Passing a house on the left, you come down to another road. Turn left here and follow this road around the Abbatiale and its farm.

6. Turn right at the road junction beside the Abbatiale to return to St. Fromond (1km approx.)

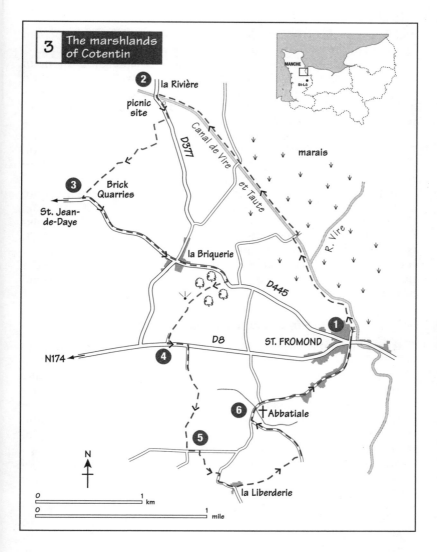

3 The marshlands of Cotentin

2 la Rivière

picnic site

Canal de Vire

D377

marais

3 Brick Quarries

St. Jean-de-Daye

la Briquerie

et Taute

R. Vire

D445

D8

ST. FROMOND

N174 ←

4

1

6 ✝ Abbatiale

5

N

0   1 km

0   1 mile

la Liberderie

More Walks in the Area

Tourist Information centres at every town in the marais can offer you free leaflets of walks in their area. In addition, there are collections of walks around Ste-Mère-Montebourg in the north, Lessay in the west and St. Jean-de-Daye in the east. The walks in each of these collections are strong on mapping and waymarking and so are easily followed – but it might be helpful to have some understanding of French in order to discover what each route has to offer. More leaflets are being produced by the minute – the area's tourist potential is expanding! There is also a variety of short 'discovery trails' where you can learn about the wildlife – again, apply to any Office du Tourisme.

From the collection *Entre Terre et Marais* in the neighbourhood of St. Jean-de-Daye, consider taking the very short walk (4km.) around Tribehou. The village is well worth visiting for its traditional dwellings and preserved flat-bottomed boat (see below), but here you also venture on to the marais itself.

Also in the collection *Entre Terre et Marais* is a circuit (11km.) starting from the interesting little town of Graignes (see below). Again on this route, you will see the red mud houses (at le Bas Vernay) and there is a long section beside the marais.

In the collection based on Ste-Mère-Montebourg, there are more routes exploring the marais based on the town of Picauville. For something a little different, also from this collection, try one of the walks based on Sainte-Marie-du-Mont, just north of Carentan on the D913. From this hill there are glorious views over the Baie des Veys, where the Vire and the Taute empty into the sea, and beyond the bay to the beaches of the *débarquement* and, in the north, to the St. Marcouf Islands.

Places of interest nearby

The park headquarters, the Manoir de Cantepie, is signed from the N13 between Carentan and Isigny – Leave at the exit Aire de Cantepie. This old 16th century farm-manor has been beautifully restored and now houses some fascinating exhibitions and film material that can be accessed in several languages. Just by pressing a few buttons you can learn about wildlife on the marais, cider production, the fishing industry, farming and dairy produce and much more of regional interest. There are books and leaflets relating to the marais, – and, indeed, to most of Normandy. The shop offers a variety of regional products, and is an ideal place to find those presents to take home. And when you have finished all that, there is a superb restaurant that specialises in regional dishes – try eel braised in pommeau!

The marais is a watery domain and is ideally seen from a boat. To explore all the possibilities, go along to the Ponts d'Ouve visitor centre, just north of Carentan (leave the N13 at the exit St. Côme du Mont and follow the signs). This discovery centre offers guided walks and bird watching as well as boat trips through the marshes in a glass-topped boat. Whole and half day boat trips are possible and bookings can be made at the Office du Tourisme at Carentan as well as at Ponts d'Ouve.

One of the most typical villages of the marais is Tribehou, west of St. Fromond. On the rue de l'Isle (and elsewhere) are several of the old *maisons torchis* – the houses made of mud and straw. In the centre of the village a shelter made of the same material houses an old *gabarre*, one of the old flat-bottomed boats that were used to transport produce. These boats were all of 17 metres long and about 4 metres wide and could be powered by sail, by towing or by 'punting' them with a long pole. There is also a short waymarked walk through the marshes starting from the church.(see above)

At Graignes, just north of Tribehou, there is a Hippodrome – a race-course devoted to the typically Norman sport of trotting. Races are held at least once a month – it's a very French experience. There is also a fine view over the marshes from the Franco-American memorial. There are more *maisons torchis* in the hamlets of le Bas Vernay and le Haut Vernay to the south and the marshes to the east are a possible place for a sighting of those storks.

4. Roches de Ham
and the valley of the Vire

In this attractive region, a rockface more than 80 metres high dominates the meandering river Vire. This walk leads you to a viewpoint on the top of the precipice and then descends to return along the old towpath beside the river.

Grade: Moderate

Distance: 10km (6¼ miles) with optional extension of 4km to la Chapelle-sur-Vire

Time: 2½ hours

Map: IGN Série Bleue 1413 O

Start and finish: The church at Mesnil-Raoult

How to get there: From St.-Lô, take the D28 south. In 9km., at St. Romphaire, turn left, S.P. to le Mesnil-Raoult. The church is on the corner ahead of you as you come into the village.

Refreshment: There is a small bar/tabac in le Mesnil-Raoult. At the Roches de Ham a little stone crêperie-cum-cider bar perches on a ledge with excellent views – but it is open only in summer.

Notes: This walk is not too demanding although there are one or two steepish climbs. It is quite suitable for trainers in dry summer weather – otherwise, boots are recommended. On a hot day it would be a good idea to carry water, although the little bar/restaurant at the Roches de Ham should be able to revive you (note that it is closed in winter). This is a figure-of-eight walk, which you might like to extend by continuing along the riverside to la Chapelle-sur-Vire (a further 2km each way). This pleasant little village (see Places of Interest) would make an ideal place to stop for lunch – either to picnic beside the river or enjoy a meal at the attractive auberge.

Waymarking: The route is waymarked in blue throughout

Introduction

The River Vire enjoys a life of contrasts. In youth it winds and tumbles through deep wooded gorges cut in a plateau of granite schist; in old age it is a wide straight channel crossing the open marais (marshland) to Isigny and the sea. Its journey between is through the heart of the Normandy countryside, a green and fertile landscape. The underlying granite causes just one more moment of drama – the outcrop known as the Roches de Ham, a sheer rock face towering 80 metres over a meander of the river. The views from the top are splendid. This was a land fought over and laid to waste a mere half century ago – St Lô to the north was completely devastated. Now plump and placid Normandy cows graze peacefully under the apple orchards and stone farms dot the landscape as far as the eye can see. In springtime, gorse

Looking down the River Vire to the Roches de Ham

and broom splash colour across the rock face and far below the river glides on in silence. Of course the site affords opportunities for rock-climbing enthusiasts – if you want action, you can go down to their platform and watch their endeavours. Apparently the rocks also house caves that once sheltered refugees from the Revolution.

The surrounding countryside is excellent for walking. The land is undulating and pleasant, with interesting villages and many good viewpoints. Beside the river it is possible to enjoy long stretches of towpath. This walk starts from the hilltop village of le Mesnil-Raoult and promptly heads downhill to meet and cross the river at the Pont de la Roque where there is a picnic area in a delightful setting. Crossing the river again, and walking through flat farm land, the surprising bulk of the Roches de Ham looms on the far bank. A little grey building crouches below the summit – the cider bar. If you would like to extend your route before climbing to the top of the Roches, you can walk beside the river to the fascinating village of la Chapelle – a place of pilgrimage for nearly a thousand years. The huge chapel dwarfs the tiny village. Here you can picnic beside the river or be tempted by the menus at the auberge before retracing your steps. The path to the top of the Roches de Ham is not too steep and the fine views await – along with refreshment. In summer this is a popular spot. But the walk continues over the summit and down to the river again, where an easy and attractive stretch on the towpath precedes the short climb back to le Mesnil-Raoult.

The Walk

1. At the road junction, face the church and take the road to the right (i.e. church on left) alongside the church. In just a few metres you will find a blue flash marked with the circuit number (here C 5 II) telling you to turn right. This sunken track leads you down to a road, where you turn left (and pick up the waymarks of a Grande Randonnée). The road leads ahead into a broad earthen track that soon doubles back on itself and runs steeply downhill to the river.

2. Cross the river on the attractive arched bridge (Pont de la Roque). There is a picnic site beside the river– but you will be returning here later. Continue on the road through the village, and at the cross-roads, turn right following blue flashes now marked C 5 I. Pass more picnic tables and again cross the river. Now follows a long flat stretch between farms, where the Roches de Ham can be seen towering over the river on the left. After about 1km., at a T-junction, turn right – there may be no waymarking here as the circuit has been re-routed. After a further 500 metres or so, turn left on the main road and continue downhill. On the right you will see signs to the Moulin Hebert, another pleasant picnic site beside the river.

3. If you wish to extend your walk to la Chapelle-sur-Vire, turn right here and bear right on the waymarked track, which is now also a Grande Randonnée. It is about 2km to la Chapelle on this pleasant track above and then beside the river and you will need to return along the same route.

To continue to the Roches de Ham, cross the river on the main road. In about 200 metres, before the road corners left, look for a track on the left. This takes you uphill through the wood, cutting off the wide bend of the road. Rejoining the road at the top, turn left, and enjoy fine views all the way to the Roches de Ham (approx. 500 metres)

4. Cross the grassy car park to find the track at the bottom right hand corner. Now you are on a ledge high above the river and a wide vista stretches before you. In summer at least, you can enjoy it all with a glass of cider. When you are ready to continue, keep ahead on the broad track marked as a Grande Randonnée. As you descend, the rock climbing platform can be reached by following the signs to the *Escalade* on the left . Continuing ahead, you can see the church and village of le Mesnil-Raoult on the hill ahead across the river. The path descends to the village of l'Angle, where you cross the river on the Pont de la Roque once more (Point 2). Now turn right beside the picnic area to reach the grassy towpath. There follows a pleasant and easy stretch beside the river for almost half an hour until you reach a canoe/kayak centre.

5. Leaving the main river, the track passes the centre headquarters on the left, and then swings left and then right below the rocks to

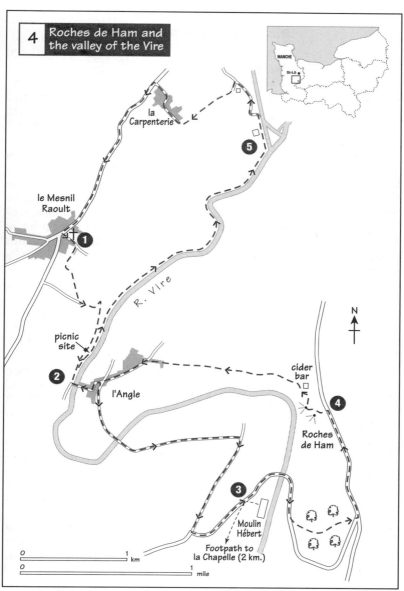

4 | Roches de Ham and the valley of the Vire

la Carpenterie

le Mesnil Raoult

1

5

R. Vire

picnic site

2

l'Angle

cider bar

4

Roches de Ham

3

Moulin Hébert

Footpath to la Chapelle (2 km.)

0   1 km

0   1 mile

reach the hamlet of la Sauvagerie. Here, turn left beside a big farmhouse, and take the narrow sunken track just to its right. The track climbs quite steeply and unfortunately can be very wet after heavy rain (it seems to be the bed of a stream). The track emerges at the top in the village of la Carpenterie, where you turn right on the road. Reaching the bigger road, turn left and follow it (with care) for about 800 metres to return to le Mesnil-Raoult

More Walks in the Area

The valley of the Vire is a superb area for walking. The upper part of the valley is in the *département* of Calvados and the lower part is in the *département* of Manche and though, in this case, the twain do meet – at Fourneaux – there is no overlap of information between the two departments. So if you want to walk the upper valley you should go to the Office de Tourisme in Vire for information, and for the lower valley, seek the same in St. Lô.

For details of the area around the Roches de Ham, in the lower valley, the very helpful Office de Tourisme at Tessy-sur-Vire may well seem preferable for on-the-spot information. Here you will find the *Guide des Sentiers Pédestres*, a well-produced booklet offering 13 walks in the area. You have seen some of their excellent waymarking on this walk. The walks in this book are accompanied by a lot of French text, but it is possible to follow each one from the map and this most reliable waymarking. The circuit from Tessy through la Chapelle is interesting in that it first follows the river for about 4km You can choose to complete the circuit (a further 11km.) or return the same way. The route passes the Grotte du Diable – see below.

For something of a change in scenery, you might consider the circuits in the south at Gouvets and St. Vigor des Monts. Gouvets is a curious and most attractive little village centred on a church surrounded by lakes with deep wooded valleys on all sides. Climbing through one of these you reach St. Vigor, its hill claiming to be the '3rd highest point in Manche'. There are picnic tables in a pleasant wooded setting, and a newly-erected orientation table. The latter is a little baffling in that it doesn't tell you what you can see – but it is quite artistic and the view is splendid in its own right.

In the upper valley (information from Vire) are the Gorges de la Vire. These deep wooded gorges offer walks in spectacular scenery – see the More Walks section of Walk 9 at le Bény-Bocage.

Going a little farther afield, *Promenades dans le bocage Saint-Lois* is a collection of 7 walks, each of which is also suitable for mountain bike, in the countryside around St.-Lô. Again there are excellent maps and first-class waymarking (all in yellow) accompanied by lots of French text, which is not essential. Try the shortish (9km.) *Circuit de la Luzerne* north-east of the town for an attractive wooded circuit – with lots of change of contour.

Places of interest nearby

In the valley of the Vire, it is well worth visiting the little village of la Chapelle-sur-Vire, even if you decide not to extend your walk that far. The chapel completely dominates the village. It has been a site of pilgrimage since the 12th century when two shepherds found in the river a statue representing St Anne carrying in her arms the Virgin and Child. As soon as the statue left the water, it apparently broke, but miraculously welded itself together again! Pilgrims since have come on foot and by boat, perhaps in the hope of similar healing. The village has an attractive auberge and the banks of the river make a pleasant picnic site. Following the road from the village in the direction of Févranches, the Grotte du Diable is signed on the left in about 300 metres. This is a purpose-built cave. Apparently in the middle 1800s, this land was bought by a Mme. Amédée Duval-Duperron whose husband then fancied the idea of a cave in which to retreat from time to time. She employed stone-cutters to carve one out of the rock high above the River Vire – the views are glorious. The cave itself seems rather less appealing.

In this region, you should not miss the opportunity to visit St-Lô – particularly on a Saturday. The town was completely destroyed during the seven-day battle for its liberation in 1944. The rebuilt town centre is now a huge square, which along with the surrounding streets, becomes each Saturday the home of an amazing market of gigantic proportions. Everything you can think of and a lot more besides is here – don't miss it!

St-Lô's other claim to fame is that it has for centuries been the home of the National Stud. There are actually 23 national studs in France, but this is one of the most important. More than a hundred stallions of several breeds live here– it is famed for its carriage horses. The stud can be visited any afternoon from June to September, with additional morning visits in July and August. On Thursday afternoons for just six weeks in summer there is a special display of horses and carriages in the courtyard.

5. The picturesque Îles Chausey

Ten miles off the west coast of Normandy lies the very beautiful archipelago of the Îles Chausey. This remote paradise has the highest rise of tide in Europe and you can take in the ever-changing views of other islands on this short ramble around the gorse-clad Grande Île.

Grade: Easy

Distance: 4km (2½ miles)

Time: Allow 2½ hours (this is a ramble!)

Map: This is not so easy. The paths are shown on a display board at the harbour or you can buy a guide book in the shop. But beware the latter – the paths shown are by no means accurate. If you can find it, you can purchase IGN Série Bleue 1214 O – or just rely on the sketch map here, you can hardly get lost.

Start and finish: The harbour on Grande Île

How to get there: By boat from the port (Gare Maritime) at Granville. There is at least one boat each way every day, and two or three daily on a summer weekend.

Refreshment: Close to the harbour are a hotel and a restaurant, both open only in the summer months (April to November approx.) The shop is open all year and sells provisions as well as souvenirs – it should be possible to rustle up a picnic.

Notes: This is a very easy and short walk – you should not need walking boots. There is little shade, so if the weather is hot you may need sun screen – and, of course, don't forget your bathing costume! And do check the time of the boat home – sometimes the published hours are altered slightly to fit in with the tide.

Waymarking: Not a lot – although there are supposed to be yellow flashes all round. But path-finding is hardly a problem.

Introduction

From the port and resort of Granville, the Îles Chausey are just a dark smudge on the horizon. The ferry boat takes about an hour to get out there, and it is a trip well worth taking. Those islands, with their golden gorse, white sand, azure sea and tropical vegetation, have just a hint of the exotic about them.

The most noticeable thing is that the views are always changing. Chausey has the highest rise of tide in Europe, almost 15 metres separating low and high water. What you see one minute is gone the next! The archipelago is said to comprise one island for every day of the year at low tide, while at high tide, you will see only one for each week. Of all these islands, only Grande Île is inhabited, and that with only a handful of souls occupied in the fishing industry. Be warned – their numbers can be increased twenty fold on a hot summer's day as the trip is quite popular. But the boats run throughout the year, and

A view across the sound

there are days in low season when you can almost imagine yourself to be Robinson Crusoe.

The Îles Chausey are in fact the southernmost islands of the Channel Island group. It is said that the islands were cut off from the mainland of Cotentin by a huge tidal wave in the autumn of 709 – but that may be more legend than fact. It seems curious that when the French took possession of Normandy in 1204, the Chausey Islands became French while the others of the group remained under English rule. Today they are administered as part of Granville, and are connected by the daily crossings.

The coastal path you follow is not exactly a demanding walk – although there are one or two short climbs. But there is a lot to see on Grande Île as well as the changing vistas to sea. The island is in fact divided in two by a low wall, one side being private and the other belonging to the state – but this seems to make little difference to where you can walk provided you are respectful. At the public end of the island there is a lighthouse on high cliffs – a lighthouse that also supplies electricity to the island. There is also a fort, built in the 1860s, now used as secondary residences for the fishing community. Below the fort is a shop open all year, and a hotel and restaurant open only in the summer months. The island's little village, Blainvillais, is in the private sector. Here are the low grey stone fishermen's cottages, and beside them, a white house once belonging to the artist Marin-Marie who settled out here. The stone farm is no longer operational – it has a long history and was once the headquarters of a smuggling ring. The path goes on beside an old chapel – with a few services still in summer – and leads up to a headland with the best views of that changing tide.

Returning south, it skirts a long sandy beach where the curious rock formations have names – the elephant and the monks are obvious ones. On the south shore of the island is the Old Fort, built in the 16th century to resist the incursions of the marauding English. It was renovated in the 1920s and became the private residence of Louis Renault of car-manufacturing fame – perhaps he needed a place where he could escape his creations. And finally, there is the beach at Port-Marie, a gorse-fringed cove of golden sand that is supervised in summertime – a safe and quite idyllic spot for a dip.

The Walk

1.   The boat will dock at either the stone slipway or the wooden landing stage depending on the state of the tide – at high tide the latter is completely submerged, while at low tide the slipway goes into the sand. Whichever way you arrive on the island, make your way uphill to a junction of paths. The shop and restaurant are just to the left here, but you turn right and pass through a gateway in a stone wall. The house that once belonged to Marin-Marie is now on your right, with the stone fishermen's cottages on the left. Continuing on the obvious path, you pass the chapel and then come to the farm on the left. Here, those yellow flashes suggest that you turn right and walk out on to the promontory in front of some low stone buildings which are now holiday gîtes. After doing this, you will find yourself directed behind the buildings to return to the main path again. At this point you should turn half right and follow the middle of the three paths, which turns left in front of a hedge.

2.   Continuing, the path now passes on the left the back gate of the Château Renault, and on the right a little harbour that opens into the Anse de Truelle. What you see here will depend on the tide – the exposed wrecks of low tide are replaced by a cove pleasant for bathing when the tide is in. Your path circles the cove, turning right to follow its farthest bank in the direction of a ruined building. This was once a boat house belonging to Louis Renault. Just before the ruins, turn and climb steeply up the hill behind to reach a house that was once a *sémaphore* – a coastguard signalling station. Here there are fine views across The Sound with its many boats at anchor, and beyond to the archipelago whose extent depends on the tide. On the far side of the *sémaphore* the path continues downhill to meet a broad track beside a wide rocky and sandy beach.

3.   If you turn right here you can follow the path to a beach with obvious evidence of past quarrying. The granite that built the edifice of Mont St. Michel came from these islands, as did the stone for the harbours at Granville and St. Malo.

   Turning left on the broad track, you skirt the beach called Grande

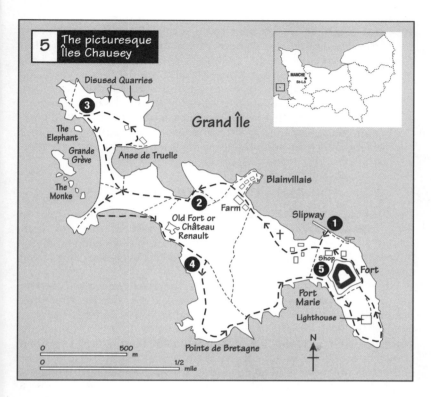

Grève. Here the three knobbly pillars out to sea (or across the beach) are termed The Monks. The large rock called The Elephant is to the right as you look seaward, but this is not the best view of it. After skirting the length of the beach, you can turn right on to a promontory, and from here the elephant shape, though distant, is a very good approximation. The path now continues along the shore of another beach, Port Homard, and then runs along the top of a wall beneath the grey walls of Château Renault. At one point you pass a rather uninviting old swimming pool that fills with the incoming tide.

4. From here the path climbs uphill and wanders on through gorse and broom. Turning right at a waymarked junction, you pass a memorial to an American aircrew who crashed on the island during the invasion of 1944. From here, continue heading out towards a concrete marker on a high point and a promontory known as the Pointe de Bretagne. The rocky peaks you can see across the sea are the Pointe de Grouin near St. Malo and the Breton coast to Cap Fréhel. After crossing more open land, you soon come to the most attractive Port-Marie where there is a fine beach with picnic tables.

5.   Cross the head of the beach and turn right on a path running below the lighthouse. Where this path forks, do not turn left uphill, but keep straight ahead and eventually you will be lead around the point on a rocky path with the lighthouse towering overhead. As you round the point there are good views of the Sound and the archipelago. Continuing ahead, the path reaches a broad track beside the fort – its old moat now makes a good grazing for goats, while inside fishermen store their equipment. From here it is only a few minutes along the track to the shop and restaurant – and the harbour.

More Walks in the Area

Unfortunately, Normandy has no other similar islands where you can walk – you will have to resort to Brittany – the Île de Bréhat is the nearest – or even sever the French connection completely and set sail for Jersey or Guernsey. Both Channel Islands are served by boat from Granville.

Should you be staying near Granville, there are two walks based on the town and you can get details of both at the Office de Tourisme. Both walks are also included in the Topoguide *La Manche à Pied (Ref. D050)*. The shorter of the walks (7km.) starts from the Office du Tourisme itself and tours the town, the beach and the long headland known as the Pointe du Roc. If you prefer something more rural, more energetic, and more than twice as long, try the second walk. It takes in a lengthy section of the coast including Granville, and also much inland countryside as well.

The Topoguide already mentioned in this section (*La Manche à Pied*) is quite a good investment if you are holidaying around here as it describes 43 circular routes, all reasonably close to Granville. It is one of the new Topoguides and the walks are very attractively presented – but it would be helpful to have some knowledge of French. Nevertheless, the maps are good and the routes themselves very well waymarked. One of the most pleasant nearby walks included in this book passes through the valley of the River Lude and then follows the Grande Randonnée along the coast south of Carolles – a total distance of 8km.

This same coastal path, the GR 223, also passes through Granville. Since Grandes Randonnées are always so well waymarked, it is easy to follow a section of this either to the north or the south of the town without even needing a map. But if you feel happier knowing exactly where you are going, the route is marked on the relevant Série Bleue maps. And for more information, there is always the Topoguide *Tour du Cotentin (Ref. 200)*. If you don't want to retrace your steps to get home, it is possible to take a bus to Carolles, and return on foot following the GR to Granville – a walk of about 4 hours along some interesting coastline. The Office du Tourisme will help you with timetables.

Places of interest nearby

Granville itself has many claims to fame, not least of which is its 4-day carnival held at the beginning of Lent. If you prefer to visit at a rather warmer time of year, there is still plenty to enjoy in this interesting town, which likes to think of itself as 'The Monaco of the North'. Above the resort areas of the beach and port is an old town with ramparts along which you can walk and enjoy the fine views to sea. Granville guards one side of the entrance to the Bay of St. Michael's Mount – and for this reason it was a prized possession of the British until the mid-1400s. The other rocky portal of the bay is the Pointe du Grouin in Brittany, and this can be clearly seen from the ramparts and from the rocky heights of the cliffs near the Pointe du Roc. The Îles Chausey can also be seen to the north-west.

If you are seeking good beaches, there are plenty more to choose from. The beach at St. Pair, just south of Granville is particularly recommended for children. Continuing south along the coast, you pass the resorts of Joullouville and Carolles before rounding the Pointe de Champeaux and getting the first views of Mont St. Michel across the water. The rise of tide in this bay is almost as great as that on Chausey, and it is said that the tide comes in here as fast as a horse can gallop. It is certainly not recommended to walk out across the sand. But if the urge to venture there is irresistible, you can always go along to Genêts, from where courageous pilgrims made the trip to Mont St. Michel in centuries past. Now the Maison de la Baie arranges expeditions across the sands and you are armed against the vagaries of the tides by guides with mobile phones.

6. The waterfalls of Mortain

Mortain was the scene of one of the most critical battles of the allied invasion of 1944. This most interesting walk, skirting the town, climbs to a viewpoint high on 'Hill 314' and descends to the valley of the Cance with its famous twin waterfalls.

Grade: Moderate

Distance: 6km (3¾ miles)

Time: 2 hours (there is lots to see!)

Map: IGN Série Bleue 1415 O. The route can also be found on the town map in the leaflet *Bonnes Vacances à Mortain* obtainable from the Office du Tourisme.

Start and finish: Parking at the Place du Château, Mortain

How to get there: The D977 from Vire passes through the town centre. After passing the Collégiale on the left (heading south), turn right where Parking is signposted.

Refreshment: Mortain has a plentiful supply of bars and restaurants. There are also two picnic table sites below the Petite Cascade.

Notes: This is a well-trodden route, which is suitable for trainers. But do not be deceived by this – the climb to the Petite Chapelle, though on roads and good tracks, is very steep, as is a later optional climb above the Grande Cascade. There is no refreshment en route so you might like to carry fluid – but it is a short walk and always within reach of the town. The view from the Petite Chapelle is fantastic on a fine day – take some binoculars!

Waymarking: The route in part follows the GR 22 with its white on red waymarks. Elsewhere it is waymarked in yellow.

Introduction

When the allied forces were sweeping through Normandy in the summer of 1944, Hitler devised a plan for a 'counter-attack', a last-ditch attempt to try to cut in two the American forces to the west. Mortain was bombed heavily for two nights before the Panzer divisions pushed forward to the town. Most of the civilian population had fled to the shelter of the iron mines at Neufbourg. A battalion of the American 30th infantry, camped on 'Hill 314' to the east of the town, were surrounded and cut off from supplies while battle raged for 6 days. They lost almost half their number, but held out – the attack was repelled and Mortain was liberated, but in ruins. The whole affair was, in fact, a military miscalculation and an event which precipitated the war's end, since most of the attacking 7th Army were shortly afterwards trapped in the 'Falaise Pocket'.

Amazingly, two of Mortain's most important buildings remained standing – the Collégiale St. Evroult, a church almost a thousand years old in the centre of town, and on the outskirts, the Abbaye Blanche,

Cloisters at the Abbaye Blanche

from virtually the same era. Both these buildings are passed on this walk, and both welcome visitors. Mortain is built on the side of a hill, and from the centre of town the walk sets out on a steep ascent to the 'Petite Chapelle' on its wooded summit. This was the hill held by the American forces and of course there is a memorial to their courage. The chapel was built in 1852 and beside it is a viewpoint – with orientation table – from which on a clear day, you can see Mont St Michel, over 40km away. This rocky ridge is actually known as 'Montjoie', since from here the pilgrims of old were pleased to catch a first glimpse of their objective, the distant abbey in its bay.

The walk continues through woods below the rocky face of the hill and then descends in the north to reach the grounds of the Abbaye Blanche. The abbey itself is most certainly grey, but it was apparently from the white habits of the monks that its name was derived. The buildings are of varied styles and ages, but the oldest date from the 13th century. The cloisters particularly are impressive. Today the abbey is the home of the Communauté des Béatitudes, who arrange visits if you apply to the reception.

From the abbey, the route swiftly descends into a rocky valley lined with rhododendrons, where the River Cance tumbles 20 metres or so in a 'Grande Cascade'. Mortain is famed for these waterfalls and they are truly picturesque. Farther on, the river Cançon, a tributary of the Cance, has cut an even deeper valley. In this gorge is the Petite Cascade, and here the little river plunges sharply on its way to round a tall pinnacle of rock known as l'Aiguille – the needle. It is a site favoured by rock climbers. Beside the confluence of the rivers is a picnic site where you could take a break before returning to town – which, very surprisingly, is merely a few minutes away.

The Walk

1. Leaving the car park at the Place du Château, walk uphill into the main street of the town. Here turn left, and then, crossing the road, turn right and climb some steps with the church (Collégiale) on your right and the Mairie on the left. Continue climbing up the Rue des Fontaines. At the top, turn right on the Rue de la 30th Division Américaine. After passing the hospital, take the first small road on the left, the Rue de Versailles. Here you meet the first yellow waymarks as you climb quite steeply again. Arriving at the top, turn right, and after about 50 metres, left on a track signposted to the Petite Chapelle. This track soon leads into pleasant woodland, where another burst of energy is required for the final ascent. Arriving at the top, the memorial to the American infantry halts you for a few moments before you turn to the chapel on the right – to see the magnificent view you will need to walk around behind it.

2. Walk away from the chapel on the broad track through the trees. You have now joined the Grande Randonnée, the GR 22, and there are white on red waymarks. Continue to the road, where there is one of the seagull pillars of the themed itinerary *La Contre-Attaque* – it again tells the story of Hill 314. Turn left on this road, and then, just before the apartment buildings, right on to a track that passes behind them – you are still following the GR. This is now an attractive path through woodland, which was somewhat devastated in the storm of December 1999. The path passes under the granite cliffs of the Rochers de Montjoie. Reaching the road at its end, continue ahead around the apartment blocks following the GR waymarks.

3. On reaching the D157, cross over, bearing right to the road opposite (signed to Tennis) This road soon begins to descend. Where the road bears right, take a road on the left, waymarked as a GR and signed to l'Abbaye Blanche. Continue ahead beside a big laurel hedge and at the bottom of the hill, enter the grounds of the abbey. Now the path bears right towards the abbey, and at its back entrance, bears left around the buildings to gain the front with its cloisters. A statue of Madonna and Child towers high on a rock above.

4. Leave the abbey and turn left on the main road. Where this bears left (150m approx.), cross the road and follow the path signed to the Grande Cascade. You descend steeply beside the waterfall and then cross the river on a long wooden footbridge. Seats are provided for you to take in the scene! Continuing on the far side, the path climbs above the river and soon you reach some metal railings. They are painted with a yellow flash. At this point the GR,

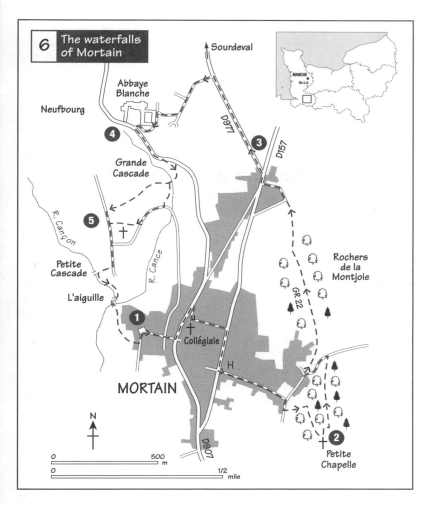

6 The waterfalls of Mortain

Sourdeval

Abbaye Blanche

Neufbourg

4

Grande Cascade

3

D157

5

R. Cançon

R. Cance

Petite Cascade

L'aiguille

Rochers de la Montjoie

GR 22

1

Collégiale

H

MORTAIN

N

0   500
         m

0   1/2
                     mile

D907

Petite Chapelle

2

marked white on red, turns sharply right between two rocks and climbs steeply up the hillside. You can choose your route – both arrive at the church at Neufbourg.

If you opt to follow the GR, you are in for another steep climb – this time on a narrow path winding over rocks and through the vegetation. But the views across the town are superb. In a clearing at the top, you turn left to the road, where you again turn left to reach the church.

The yellow marked route climbs rather more gently. To take this, continue on the path to the road. Here turn right, and after 200 metres or so, bear right on an uphill track signed to the 12th century church at Neufbourg. Continue past the church to meet the road and turn left.

5. Whichever route you chose to reach the church, continue now downhill on the road. The GR leaves via a road on the right, but you continue for about 200 metres to a road on the right banded in yellow and white and signed to the Petite Cascade. Before the bridge and the lavoir, turn left on a very pretty path that descends beside the waterfall, and follows beside the river through its deep gorge. The rock known as l'Aiguille dominates the scene on the opposite bank. Passing through the picnic area beside the mingling rivers, continue ahead over the bridge. A final climb beneath another granite face returns you to the Place du Château

More Walks in the Area

The Office de Tourisme in Mortain has produced its own walking brochure *Ballades Mortainaises*. This inexpensive little booklet details 8 walks in the immediate vicinity of Mortain. The first of these is the route described here. Each walk has a detailed route description and lots of information, but although the maps with these walks are easily followed, you will sadly miss out on all the text if you do not have some knowledge of French. If you decide to try it, Circuit no. 5 (Le Neufbourg – St. Barthélémy – Bellefontaine) is interesting. Bellefontaine makes a pleasant half-way stop and you could visit the *Village Enchanté* (see below). On the return there are fine views of the valley of the River Sée. The total distance is 12km, and you follow the GR 22 all the way back from Bellefontaine to Mortain.

Following a GR is addictive and it is quite possible to follow this one (GR 22) through to Avranches – a distance of about 70km – and indeed on to Mont St. Michel. There are also several other *Grandes Randonnées du Pays* in this region – these are long circuits (70 – 150km.) which would take several days. All this is possible if you have the use of two cars – or any Office du Tourisme would be able to advise you about taxis. These routes are all described in the Topoguide *La Manche à Pied (Ref. D050)*.

Moving away from Mortain, the valley of the Sée just to the north is an excellent area for walking. The upper part of the valley near Sourdeval perhaps suffers from some industrial invasion, but lower down is deep green glorious countryside with many walks in the area. A series of routes, *Les Randonnées de la Sée*, has been produced and is available from the Office du Tourisme at Sourdeval. Here is a handful of walks that you can follow from their waymarking alone if you cannot understand the relatively easy French. Accompanying the routes are sketch maps, which, although quite good, might make you think of acquiring the IGN map of this region (1415 O). The walk *Circuit de la Sée* that starts from Brouins is an excellent choice from the above series. Just 10km in length, it crosses the river beside an eco-museum and climbs to Perriers-en-Beaufficel, a village with outstanding views over the valley. Descending again, it follows beside the river on an old railway track for some 3km before returning to Brouins.

Finally, la Fosse Arthour, an attractive gorge in the Regional Natural Park is a mere 18km from Mortain – see Walk 4 in this book.

Places of interest nearby

Bellefontaine, mentioned in the other walks section, has an interesting natural park known as the Village Enchanté. It is ideal for children, having a valley of fairy stories, model theatre, tourist train and lots more. The park is open every day from Easter to September

Just a little further north is the village of St. Michel de Montjoie, perched on its granite promontory with distant views to Mont St. Michel. This seems an appropriate location for the interesting Museum of Granite, which displays the history of quarrying and the many uses of the material in both outdoor and indoor settings. The museum is open every afternoon in July and August, and Sunday afternoons only in the other summer months

If you decide to venture into the valley of the Sée mentioned in the previous section, you could visit the Eco-museum at Brouins, where the story of migrating Atlantic Salmon is mixed with that of the coming of the Paper Mills to the upper valley and the production of cutlery. The museum is open daily during the summer months and afternoons only at some other times.

And yet another museum – of a more practical sort– is La Maison de la Pomme et de la Poire near Barenton (10km south-east). The story of cider and the delicious poiré is told in farm buildings and an orchard – and is followed by a tasting session. Open every day in summer.

Mortain is on the themed itinerary *La Contre-Attaque*, one of a series of eight routes that follow chronologically the events of the summer of 1944. *La Contre-Attaque* runs from Alençon to Avranches and visits sites and memorials associated with this fated military action. For more information and a brochure on all these routes, contact the Fédération Nationale des Comités Départementaux de Tourisme, 2, rue Linois, 75015 Paris.

7. The legendary site of the Fosse Arthour

King Arthur and Queen Guinevere are apparently trapped beneath the rocky slabs of this gorge. Not to worry – the Fosse Arthour is a most attractive spot to visit and this walk also includes some stunning views from the hills above it.

Grade: Moderate

Distance: 7km (4½ miles)

Time: 2½ hours

Map: IGN Série Bleue 1415 E

Start and finish: Parking at the Vieille Auberge of the Fosse Arthour

How to get there: From the D907 between Mortain and Domfront, turn north in the village of St.-Georges-de-Rouelley (S.P. to Fosse Arthour). At the fork in 3km., turn right to the Auberge of the Fosse.

Refreshment: The Vielle Auberge is at the entrance to the Fosse. It is a large alpine-style stone building offering everything from snacks to dinner dances.

Notes: This is a walk on good paths, which in summer could be suitable for trainers, but it does include some fairly steep climbing in the first part. You would be advised to carry fluid as there is no refreshment en route. You might also like to take binoculars for the distant views.

Waymarking: The route is waymarked in yellow, except for the valley path, which is a Grande Randonnée (marked white on red)

Introduction

It all resulted from an infringement of the rules of the valley. King Arthur and his Queen had separate rooms on either side of the river. The genie of the valley had forbidden Arthur to cross over until after the sun had set. One day Arthur decided to defy him. A huge torrent arose and swept Arthur into a chasm beneath a fall of rock. His devoted Queen threw herself after him. Now they apparently sleep on in their subterranean chambers, the exits forever closed by the fallen boulders at the entrance to this valley.

Nevertheless, the sheer rock faces on either side of the river here offer good opportunities for local climbing groups. The area is part of the Natural Regional Park of Normandie-Maine, a park covering the largely forested territory of the south of Normandy. The Fosse has become a leisure centre where it is possible to go pony trekking, to hire mountain bikes, to fish in the river or to take out pedalos on the lake. All this takes place in the setting of a picturesque wooded valley where a bubbling stream bounces merrily over the boulders – the huge grey rock faces are features only of its entrance.

Having a 'family day out' sort of atmosphere, at least in summer-time, you are likely to share the valley path with quite a few other amblers. But the walk described here first leads you away, and begins quite energetically, climbing to the heights way above the Fosse. Indeed, very soon you are way above just about everything else as well. The views are tremendous. Normandy cows graze on sloping pastures beside grey stone farmhouses, totally unaware of their privileged surroundings. When at length your way turns downhill again, you pass through a rural scene of farms and orchards before joining the GR 22 to enter the wooded valley of the Fosse. Wherever there is a feature of interest, there will be a Grande Randonnée to take you there! These beech and oak woods are particularly splendid in Autumn and all too soon you arrive at civilisation in the form of the fishing lake. Beyond are the crumbled rock faces – Queen Guinevere's chamber on the right, King Arthur's on the left as you leave the valley of the Fosse Arthour.

Path beside the River Sonce, Fosse Arthour

The Walk

1. Pass the Vielle Auberge and cross the River Sonce to enter the Fosse Arthour. The road immediately sweeps around to the left and you keep to it, following the yellow waymarks. Do not cross the river again, but keep straight ahead. Soon the road begins to climb quite steeply and there are good views back down the valley. On reaching the stone farmhouse, turn left to pass between the buildings. The route now climbs sharply on a very stony lane and enters woodland. At the top of the slope, turn left

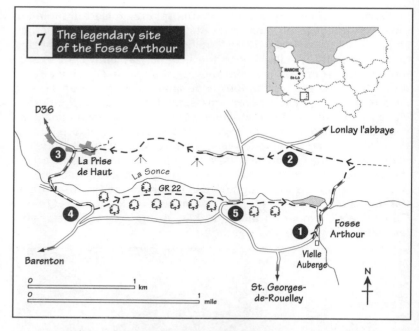

on a wide track, which crosses farmland and passes farm buildings before reaching a tarmacked road at a corner.

2. The yew tree on this corner is many hundreds of years old. Do not join the road here, but bear left on a track around the building. The path now begins to descend beside a low stone wall. The route is obvious and well-waymarked. On reaching a wide tar- macked road you cross straight over to take the road opposite, sign-posted to le Moulin-Foulon. Once again, this is a fairly steep climb. The path becomes rougher as you pass behind the lovely stone buildings at La Fieffe-Jouguet. Farther on the views appear as you pass between open fields. The clear path continues past several desirable properties, all enjoying the distant panorama. Cows and pigs graze the fields in complete oblivion. Eventually a track junction is reached and you turn downhill to pass through the farm buildings of La Prise-de-Haut.

3. Reaching the tarmacked road, turn left downhill. Several farms are passed as you follow the road through this quiet valley. After crossing the river, the road climbs gently.

4. At the summit, as the road swings right, take a track on the left, now following the white on red waymarks of the GR. The track continues into a fine wood of beech and oak, with the river below and to the left. At a track junction, you keep straight ahead, fol-

lowing the excellent waymarking of the GR. The track follows the woodland edge and there are good views of the path you took earlier, now high above you. After 20 minutes or so of walking, the track climbs to meet the road:

5. Turn left on the road, and just before the bridge, continue ahead to again enter the Fosse Arthour. The path now runs beside the lake with picnic tables and children's playground.. At its end you again encounter the massive slabs of rock– Guinevere's chamber is on this side of the river, while crossing the wooden bridge brings you beside that of Arthur. Retrace your steps to the right to reach the welcoming auberge.

More Walks in the Area

The Fosse Arthour is in the Natural Regional Park of Normandy-Maine whose headquarters is at Carrouges, east of Bagnoles-de-l'Orne. Here there are maps and routes of all kinds, covering a vast area, which is mostly forested. Nearer to hand is Domfront (10km approx.), where the Office de Tourisme has a selection of more local walks.

Just to the north of the Fosse Arthour is the little town of Ger, for centuries known for its pottery making. An 18km route from here (which can be shortened) passes the regional museum of pottery and continues through the Forêt de la Lande Pourrie. Hills, woodland, streams and villages make an interesting tour just within the boundary of the regional park. The Office de Tourisme at Domfront has details, and the walk is also included in the Topoguide *La Manche à Pied*.

Topoguides tend to collect together the very best walks in a region, and *La Manche à Pied* describes another walk not far away, this time just outside the park boundary. It starts from le Fresne-Poret, north-west of Ger, and is in some ways similar to the last – 18km as before, but rather more strenuous. However, this is fine walking country and there are good views over the valley of the Sée from le Mont-au-Loup (Wolf Hill). Coincidence or not, this overlooks the ruins of le Prieuré de Moutons (Priory of Sheep) – a one-time religious foundation for women! Its octagonal fountain and a stone cross are still to be seen.

If the GR 22 has inspired you to follow it farther into the Park, another Topoguide, *Tour dans le Parc Normandie-Maine* might help with routes. The Office de Tourisme at Domfront could advise about travel.

And finally, consider visiting Mortain (18km west) and taking Walk 3 – it is a place full of interest and the Tourist Office here can offer you many more walks in this region.

Places of interest nearby

Domfront, 10km east of the Fosse, is an interesting old town which has preserved vestiges of its 11th century fortifications. It is the capital of the *Passais* country, known for pear-growing.

On the D907 near the village of Barenton, is the *Maison de la Pomme et de la Poire*. This aims to tell you everything there is to know about the production of cider and its pear equivalent, *poiré* (perry) – not forgetting pommeau and calvados. The visit ends with a tasting session and regional products are on sale.

At le Placître, just west of Ger, is the *Musée Régional de la Poterie*. The site is certainly extensive – it comprises more than a dozen restored old buildings among which are three kilns, the workshop, the potter's house and a pottery exhibition. Touring all this takes a little while, and you will be pleased to find refreshment available at the central cafeteria. The museum is open in afternoons only in the summer months.

Cider apples

Calvados

8. Views of Port Winston at Arromanches

The concrete blocks of the Mulberry harbour out to sea at Arromanches are a most tangible reminder of the D-Day landings. You can see them from near and far when you take this walk through the green valley behind the town.

Grade: Easy

Distance: 15km (9½ miles). But it is possible to take just a short circuit of about 6km (3¾ miles)

Time: 4 hours for full walk, about 1¾ hours for short circuit.

Map: IGN Série Bleue 1512 O

Start and finish: Museum of the D-Day Landings (Musée du Débarquement) at Arromanches

How to get there: Arromanches is on the coast north-west of Caen. The Musée du Débarquement is on the sea-front – and is well-signed all over the town. There is parking in front of the museum, but this can be very busy in season. Other car parks are signed at the west end of the town. All car parks may make a charge in season.

Refreshment: The narrow main street of Arromanches is crowded with restaurants and bars of all kinds. There is a pleasant little *auberge* in the village of Ryes, about half-way round the walk.

Notes: This is a longish but not-too-demanding walk. Most of it is on field tracks and sunken lanes – by all means wear your trainers in summer, but at other times the long grass can be wet and the tracks muddy, so go for boots. There is little shade on the route so you may well need sun-screen on a hot day – and perhaps you should also carry fluid, although you should be able to get a drink (and food) at Ryes. And don't forget binoculars for the views of Port Winston, and possibly a swimming costume for a dip at the end of the day.

If you opt for the short circuit, it might be worth climbing the hill past point 6 for some excellent views.

Waymarking: This walk has sections on a Grande Randonnée (GR 223), waymarked in white on red, sections on a Grande Randonnée du Pays (Tour du Bessin), waymarked in yellow on red and other sections merely waymarked in yellow. The text will tell you what to look out for.

Introduction

The troops arriving on the landing beaches on D-Day needed back-up – tanks and armoured vehicles, continuing food supplies and ammunition. It would be many days before they could even hope to capture a port. It was Churchill's conception to take a port with them – a port that could be based off a sandy beach, a port whose landing stages

The harbour at St. Vaast-la-Hougue (walk 2)

A ferry boat waiting in The Sound, Îles Chausey (walk 5)

Violets growing on the banks, Nez de Jobourg (walk 1)

Marsh marigolds on the Marais du Cotentin (walk 3)

Half-timbered farm with orchard, La Ferrière (walk 18)

'Colombage' and apple trees, The Auge (walk 10)

Relics of 'Port Winston' in the bay at Arromanches (walk 8)

Porte d'Aval and The Needle (walk 22)

Seafront at Arromanches

could rise up and down with the tide. Arromanches-les-Bains was its chosen site.

More than a year before D-Day, divers off Arromanches undertook the necessary measurements. Hollow concrete blocks the size of five-storey buildings were to be constructed and then towed across the channel, filled with water and sunk. Amazingly, German intelligence never picked up their building sites. On the chosen day, violent and unseasonal storms raged along the channel coast and the landings had to be postponed for 24 hours. D-Day was now the 6th June. The blocks were taken across a day later, still in high seas, and several were lost en route. Once in place, the rough waves damaged yet more. The companion American harbour on Omaha beach was completely destroyed by more storms two weeks later. But the port at Arromanches functioned, and soon 7,000 tonnes of supplies a day were landing that way. The port of Cherbourg did not become functional until August – and the rest, as they say, is history.

The blocks were not immediately removed at the end of the war. In time, several were taken for reconstructions in Paris and others were used to block a breach in the dykes of Holland. But the rest remained in the seas off Arromanches and you can see them today. The D-Day museum on the sea front is something of a pilgrimage site. Its windows look out across the sea with its memories while multilingual guides tell the story using working models. On the cliff above, a new Cinema 360° takes you to the heart of the battle.

In Arromanches you will no doubt want to visit these sites – and this walk passes the Cinema 360° as it leaves the town. From the cliff-top there is perhaps the best view over the bay, still ringed by the harbour remains. But the walk then takes you away from the crowds up a wide green valley between fields of corn. This was the land they fought over – the stark cemeteries lie in the villages around. The valley is long and when you arrive at the village of Ryes you can find refreshment at a little auberge. From there the route heads up the hill behind the church and from the grassy track at the top you again have superb views over the bay with its memorials – views that will stay with you all the way as you follow a succession of lanes back to Arromanches.

The Walk

1. Leaving the Musée du Débarquement , keep the sea on your left and walk up the hill towards the Cinema 360° on the cliff ahead, passing an old Sherman tank on the way. Here you are on the route of the GR 223 and can follow the white on red waymarks. Cross the grass on the top of the hill (Arromanches is very photogenic from here) and continue across the car park, passing the orientation table. At the far end of the car park, continue ahead, walking parallel to the road (the GR leaves you and crosses the road here) and passing the reservoir. Finally joining the road, turn left and walk downhill.

2. Take the first road on the left (now waymarked in yellow) towards some seaside houses in the village of la Fontaine St. Côme. At its end, turn right and the right again to return to the main road. At this road, cross straight over (S.P. to the Mairie) and continue ahead following the yellow waymarks.

3. On reaching the cross roads with the main road (D 65)

For the Short Cut:

Turn right along this road for about 30 metres, and then turn left up the track beside the farm. Now see Point 6 – and consider walking up the hill a little for the view.

For the Main Walk:

Turn left, and at the cross-roads in about 100 metres, keep straight ahead. A little farther on, look for a wooden signpost directing you left beside a stone wall on a narrow path.

4. Coming shortly to a track T-junction, turn right on a broad cross-field path towards the village of Asnelles. In the middle, near a concrete telegraph pole, you will need to zig-zag to the left a little (i.e. turn left then immediately right). This path brings you in to a narrow road in the village. Now keep your eyes open for an alley between walls on the right, the Sentier au Bâtard – it is waymarked in yellow on red. The alley becomes a path, which continues between fields and over a stream before reaching a tarmacked road. Here turn right, then keep right at the fork (follow-

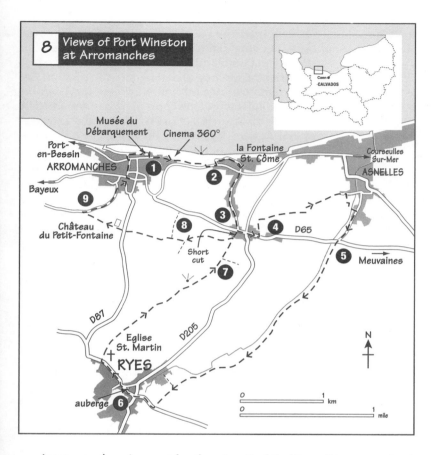

ing a wooden signpost for the circuit of the Port d'Arromanches) and continue ahead to the main road.

5. Cross straight over this road to a rough track opposite, now waymarked in yellow. Now keep ahead on this track with the little River Gronde on your right for about 4km., ignoring all side tracks. On reaching a tarmacked road, turn right into the village of Ryes. (The yellow waymarking is a little confusing around here. You may have noticed a yellow-flashed track going off on the right before you reached the tarmacked road. Once at the road, the track opposite bears flashes of yellow. The reason for this is that this walk has been published – and waymarked – by two different authorities, and they use different routes to circumnavigate the village of Ryes. It seems preferable to choose neither. This route goes straight through the village – at least you can stop at the auberge for a drink!)

6. On reaching the main road (the D 205) in Ryes, cross straight over to a road opposite. Keeping to the left, in about 200 metres or so you will reach a road junction. The Auberge des Monts is now just behind you on the right. Continue ahead (ignore the road on the left) towards the church of Saint-Martin. Now take the track on the right that climbs uphill behind the church – it is waymarked in yellow on red. At the fork at the top of the hill, bear right and continue on a waymarked grassy track along the top of the hill. There are fine views of the bay as you begin to descend.

7. Heading downhill you reach a signpost at the junction of the Grande Randonnée 223 and the GRP 1 and 2 (Randonnées du Pays). Continue downhill, now following the white on red waymarks of GR 223. Coming down to the farm, turn left (the short cut joins here) and keep ahead on the broad track.

8. After about 1km on this track, you reach a junction where the GR turns right. You also turn right here, but in about 250 metres, at a second junction, you leave the GR (it turns right) and continue ahead on a path that leads down to the road. Cross the road directly to the yellow-waymarked track opposite. This runs alongside the Château du Petit-Fontaine and dips into a valley to cross a stream before climbing steeply uphill again.

9. Coming out to a farm road at the top, turn right and continue down to the water tower, where you turn left and then right to return to the sea front.

More Walks in the Area

Arromanches is on the Côte de Nacre –the Mother of Pearl Coast – which stretches from the mouth of the Orne at Ouistreham to Isigny-sur-Mer. This is, of course, the scene of the D-Day landings and the beaches of Sword, Juno, Gold and Omaha succeed each other as you walk west. Only Utah is missing – it is just round the corner on the east coast of the Cotentin peninsula. This is in some ways a sad land with its many cemeteries and memorials but it is also a beautiful coastline and the GR 223 follows it closely from Arromanches to the west. Whether it is military history or just sea breezes that appeal to you, it will make an interesting walk. The route of the GR is indicated on the Série Bleue maps and, beside the one mentioned above, you will need one other – 1411 S. Grandes Randonnées are so well marked on the ground that, with the help of a map, you should have no trouble whatsoever in following this one. Heading west from Arromanches, you will pass the battery at Longues and some high cliffs before reaching the interesting fishing village of Port-en-Bessin (11km.) Another 7km or so along Omaha beach will bring you to Colleville-sur-Mer with its memorial and cemetery. A memorial and viewing table at St Laurent bring you on to Vierville and about 10km west of this is the

Point du Hoc where bunkers and craters in the ground remind you of the terrible battle fought here. A little farther on is the fishing port of Grandchamp-Maisy. There are splendid views all the way. If you do not have access to two cars for this linear walk, the Tourist Information at Arromanches (across the car park from the museum) should be able to help you find a taxi.

The fertile plain behind these beaches is known as the Bessin – and it is an area well-endowed with waymarked circular routes. The Office de Tourisme at Arromanches can offer you two leaflets of these circuits – one covering the west of the region, the other the east (Arromanches is just in the east.) You should have no trouble following these routes – the minimal French text on the leaflets relates largely to churches, chateaux, etc. en route. For a dip into wartime history, take the Circuit de la Plage d'Omaha (15km.). For an interesting port, some high cliffs and a river curiously disappearing underground, try the Circuit de Port-en-Bessin (20km.)

In addition to these leaflets, you will also find the Office de Tourisme stocked with folders of walks. The local folder is entitled *Randonnées dans le Bessin* – Canton de Ryes. Here you have 11 walks with excellent maps and French text. Some of them overlap the routes in the leaflet of the eastern region (hence the excess of yellow waymarks on the Arromanches route) and some are reproduced (at least approximately) in the Topoguide of the area, *Le Calvados à pied*. And to add to all that, there is another Topoguide devoted entirely to this region – *Tour du Bessin (Ref. 141)* – in which, in addition to circuits, you are offered a complete regional tour. As you can see, walking is given a high profile round here.

Places of interest nearby

This whole area bears testimony to the historic events of the summer of 1944. In Arromanches, the Musée du Débarquement is a must, even though the summer crowds can be a bit daunting. A discussion of the construction of the harbour with working models is followed (or preceded) by a short film of the landings. A joint ticket will then take you into the Cinema 360° on the cliff above. Here the war footage is interspersed with shots of Normandy today, prosperous, green and fertile. Was it done to extend the time (the whole show only takes 18 minutes) or underline the contrast? Whatever, it makes a strangely moving combination.

Le Mémorial at Caen was opened in 1988 as a 'Museum for Peace'. It takes things a bit farther by inviting you to reflect on all the conflicts of the 20th century – naturally with special reference to the local events of the last world war, which here are seen from both sides. Using advanced audio-visual techniques and archive film footage it makes an unforgettable impact.

With your ticket to Le Mémorial it is also possible to book a guided tour of the landing beaches. Of course you can visit the Pointe du Hoc, Omaha Beach, the Military Cemetery at Colleville and the Battery at Longues-sur-Mer under your own steam, but more can be learned from a guide and there are tours in English. If you are a fluent French speaker you can conduct yourself around the principal sites using a cassette and map bought from the Mémorial – but so far there is no English version.

It is possible to pursue the progress of the invasion throughout Normandy by following the eight themed itineraries devised to commemorate its 50th anniversary. You have no doubt seen the sea-gull logo posts, each one describing local events – ask at the Office du Tourisme for more details.

And thinking of a different invasion, Arromanches is only 10km from Bayeux, home of the tapestry commemorating the events of 1066. This is not just some piece of medieval needlework, but a complete history lesson set in a cartoon strip of 11th-century life. The film preceding the actual viewing is helpful – you are taken right through the story and so, among the hundreds of characters portrayed on 70 metres of tapestry, you know just where to find Halley's comet and Mont St. Michel, Odo the Bishop and Harold with an arrow in his eye.

9. Le Bény-Bocage and the valley of the Souleuvre

The attractive little town of le Bény-Bocage is the starting point for this walk over the green hills to the remote wooded valley of the River Souleuvre. From its old viaduct 60 metres high, bungee-jumpers leap to dip their heads in the river beneath.

Grade: Moderate.

Distance: 8km (5 miles) with optional 2km extra to visit the viaduct.

Time: 2½ hours

Map: IGN Série Bleue 1414 E

Start and finish: Place des Halles, le Bény-Bocage

How to get there: le Bény-Bocage lies just west of the D577, 10km north of Vire. The Place des Halles is the central square.

Refreshment: Le Bény-Bocage is well-provided for with at least two bar/restaurants and a hotel. There is also a restaurant at the bungee-jumping site.

Notes: There are no really difficult sections on this walk, although there are a few climbs. The valley path can be muddy in winter or after heavy rain, so at such times, walking boots would be advantageous. Most of the route is through woodland, which should offer shade in hot weather. Although the route as described does not pass the viaduct, it is easy to visit it by continuing ahead on the riverside path for a further kilometre. Once there, a sharp climb will take you to the catwalk and platform on the pillars.

Waymarking: The route is waymarked in yellow throughout (with a short section on the GR 221 in white/red)

Introduction

The word bocage appears in the names of several towns in this region of Normandy. It can be translated simply as countryside, but it really infers countryside of a particular sort – a landscape of enclosed fields and scattered woodland. Around the fields are high earthen banks planted with trees and between the banks are sunken lanes. Most of northern and western France has countryside of this sort, but it is the area centred on St.-Lô and Vire that is known as the Bocage Normande.

Le Bény-Bocage is an interesting town set in the most attractive part of this region. Granite buildings group around a central square decked with flowers. A nearby covered hall dates from medieval times. The church with its curious 'minaret-style' tower was built by one Gaston de Renty, something of a philanthropist, who was born in the château at Bény-Bocage in 1611. The story is told about his one-time visit to the other local landowner, the Count of Forêt-Vassy.

Medieval covered hall at le Bény-Bocage

The Count was a keen huntsman whose pride and joy was his pack of hounds. 'I have a finer pack', Renty told him, and invited him to come and see. The count did – and when the door was opened, the stable was seen to be full of the local poor to whom bread was being distributed. 'These are my pack' said Renty, 'and they are better than yours, since they are made in the image of God!'

This walk from le Bény-Bocage starts out on the rue Gaston de Renty. It is a road climbing steeply uphill to a fine viewpoint at la Bruyère. Above the town you are on a granite plateau of the bocage, a plateau through which streams have carved deep wooded valleys. Between these, the green fields rise steeply, and at times the views have an almost alpine feel. In the deepest valley of all, the River Souleuvre bubbles and tumbles on its way to join the Vire and a winding path follows it through the woodland. Beside the remote ruins of an old water-mill you have a choice – turn homeward peacefully, or continue beside the river for a further kilometre or so to a sight that somewhat shatters the rural idyll.

The viaduct over the Souleuvre was built in 1889 to carry the Vire – Caen railway 60 metres high above this valley. The architect was Gustave Eiffel – of tower fame. Just over a hundred years later, the line closed and only the huge pillars of the viaduct were left standing. A platform was built out from one of them and this quiet lonely valley became the first bungee-jumping site in Europe. It is terrifying to watch – and hear – these 'elastonauts' hurling themselves into the void on a piece of elastic measured so exactly that their heads do not quite reach the shallow bed of the Souleuvre. If you need more excitement you can climb to the top where – for a small sum – you are allowed to venture on to the platform. But you may prefer to quickly turn your back and return along the riverside, where you can once more be engulfed by sylvan tranquillity on the way back to le Bény-Bocage.

The Walk

1. From the Place des Halles, take the rue Gaston de Renty, which heads steeply uphill. On the way up you will notice the first white on red markings of the GR 221. At the top of the hill is the picnic area and viewpoint of la Bruyère. Turn left in front of this area and still following the GR, take the path downhill to meet the D109, where you cross straight over. Continue ahead to meet another tarmacked road.

2. Turn left on this road, and after about 30 metres, take the track on the right waymarked in yellow. The GR leaves you here and goes on down the road. Now following the yellow waymarks (as you will all the way), you keep ahead, leaving the main track, which goes downhill on the left. Soon you pass a wood on the right, and can see a coniferous wood across to the left. The track reaches a tarmacked road in the hamlet of Drouard. Just before this meets the main road, turn left on the farm track, and then right across the front of the farm. This path soon becomes a sunken track (*chemin creux*) which descends to a stream in the depths of the valley. After a steep climb, you reach a tarmacked road.

3. Cross straight over the road to a track almost opposite. Continue on this path which descends, giving you the first glimpses of the valley of the Souleuvre ahead. At a T-junction of tracks, turn left, and shortly reaching another T-junction, left again. Now the track climbs again and curves around to reach a tarmacked road in the hamlet of le Bois Pépin. Follow the road ahead for a few metres (do not turn left) and, passing a house on the right, keep ahead to a track junction.

4. Here turn right following the yellow waymarks and a signpost directing you to the valley of the Souleuvre. The path descends with good views over this lonely valley. Soon you cross the river itself on a metal bridge, and continue on a path through the trees alongside the river. Just after the ruins of the Moulin de Cervelle, another bridge comes into view.

5. If you wish to visit the site of the viaduct, continue ahead on this riverside path for another kilometre or so. You will need to return on the same route.

   To return to le Bény-Bocage, cross the bridge and bear right. Continuing on this path, you can just glimpse the viaduct on the right down the valley. At the fork, keep ahead. The path crosses an

entrant stream and then, just before another stream, you turn
sharp left uphill – it is well-waymarked. The path now climbs out
of this very pretty valley beside and above this stream. A stream
arriving from the left is crossed on a wooden plank bridge and you
continue ahead, still climbing. At the hamlet of la Vallée Surville,
your path becomes a tarmacked road. On reaching theD56, turn
left and follow this main road (with care) for about 700 metres to
reach the Place des Halles.

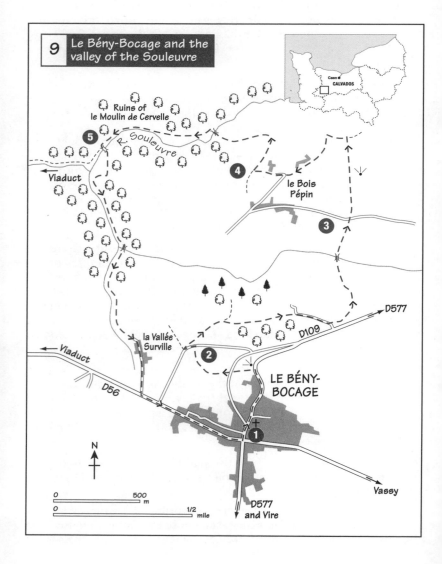

More Walks in the Area

The valleys of the Vire and the Souleuvre make excellent walking country – little-known and away from the usual tourist routes, the scenery here is pleasantly varied and even in places, quite dramatic. The gorges of the Vire and the rocky outcrops above the deep valley of the Souleuvre are well worth some exploration. There is enough here for more than a week's holiday.

The Office de Tourisme in Vire (beside the car park in the central square) should be able to offer you a variety of walking guides. One which covers just about everywhere and is reasonably priced is *Randonnées dans le Bocage de la Vire à la Souleuvre*. All the walks described in this book are well-waymarked, and the maps are very clear, enabling you to get around without recourse to the directions. But if you can manage a little French, the text contains a lot of interesting information.

From the 21 circular walks offered, it is difficult to pick out the best, but you should not miss the Gorges of the Vire. The river descends in wide loops, and at every bend, a steep cliff is opposed by a gentle slope. Fine woods of oak and beech clothe the valley and it is a wonderful sight in the autumn. A walk of 10km starts from the village of Bures-les-Monts and follows the GR 221 through a particularly winding section of the gorge. Higher up the valley is the town of Campeaux. This is the start of a 13km walk that, in the river section, passes several old water-mills. Both these routes also appear in the Topoguide *Le Calvados à Pied (Ref. D 014)*, which, although more expensive, you might like to consider if you are thinking of walking farther afield in the region.

In the same book, *Randonneées dans le Bocage de la Vire à la Souleuvre*, there is a fine long (22km.) walk from the village of Montchauvet – an excellent walk for a full day's excursion. The most exciting part of this walk follows a ridge high above the River Souleuvre with some magnificent views, but there are also woods, moors, streams and some ancient megaliths en route.

Places of interest nearby

If you are looking for a pleasant picnic spot after your walk from le Bény-Bocage, follow the signs to the *Plan d'Eau* (south of the town). This is simply a lake (regrettably only for boating, not swimming) surrounded by beautiful shrubberies and fine lawns. For young children, there is a playground, and for those a bit older, a Parcours Sportif (fitness course). The most sophisticated attraction is the mini-golf.

If you have not extended your walk to see the viaduct, you can reach it by turning west on the D56 and following the signs. The viaduct is accessible on both sides of the valley, but the bungee-jumping site is on the north side. The south side may well give you a better view – follow the signs, park your car and walk down. There is a picnic site at the bottom and from the little bridge across the river you can see it all. To visit the site itself, turn right off the D56 after crossing the river. There is a charge for parking which then allows you access. To get the best view of the jumping, you will need to pay a little more and have nerves of steel to cross the catwalk to the platform – alternatively, you can watch it on closed-circuit television in the shop. . Bungee-jumping generally takes place on weekends and holidays between March and November, but every day in July and August.

Two nearby museums are worth a mention, the first of them relating to wartime. In the allied invasion of 1944, the bocage was a land much fought over. The high banks and sunken roads proved difficult for armoured vehicles, and fighting was often hand-to-hand. Eventually the Americans came up with the 'rhinoceros', a tank with a snout that ripped through bank, trees, roots and everything. The story of the war in the bocage is told in the museum La Percée du Bocage at Saint-Martin-des-Besaces, 12km north of le Bény-Bocage. The museum is open morning and afternoon in the summer months – but closed on Tuesdays.

Continuing north on the D53 for a further 12km from Saint-Martin-des-Besaces will bring you to Caumont l'Éventé. Here there is a rather original museum known as the Souterroscope. In essence, you are guided through the tunnels of an old slate quarry, where illuminated caves tell you of the lives of the former miners, and something of the geology and natural history of this underground world. This popular attraction is open throughout the year (except Mondays in winter) and is accompanied by restaurant/bar/crêperie, picnic areas, mini-golf, etc.

10. The Auge – a land of plenty!

The countryside here has all that we think of as Normandy – half-timbered houses, cattle grazing in apple orchards, high-banked tracks and lots of wild flowers. Add some fine views and a pleasant auberge and you have the recipe for a first-class day's walk.

Grade: Moderate

Distance: 12km (7½ miles). A short cut can reduce this distance by about 4km.

Time: 3½ hours

Map: IGN Série Bleue 1713 O

Start and finish: The calvary at the crossroads in the village of St. Martin-de-Fresnay

How to get there: Follow the D40 south-east from St. Pierre-sur-Dives for a distance of about 8km.. The cross-roads is at the far end of St. Martin-de-Fresnay, before the river bridge.

Refreshment: There is a bar/restaurant /auberge in St. Martin-de-Fresnay, near the cross-roads, and another in the village of le Billot. Le Billot also has a pleasant picnic site with a view. More picnic tables are sited beside the River Oudon, just out of St. Martin-de-Fresnay.

Notes: This is a walk with a few steep climbs, mostly on hollowed out tracks. These are not normally a problem, but after heavy rain – beware! Water can pour down them and it can seem that you are walking on the bed of a stream. At other times the *cavées* can be muddy, although fine summer weather should make the route quite suitable for trainers. The easy short cut misses out the attractive half-timbered village of le Billot.

Waymarking: The route is well-waymarked – but remember to keep changing colour: 1 – 2 white; 2 – 3 yellow on red; 3 – 6 blue; 6 – 7 yellow on red; 7 – 1 white

---

Introduction

From the Auge comes all the bounty of Normandy. Here the grass is greener, the apple trees more heavily laden, the black-and-white speckled cows yet more contented. It is a land flowing with milk and honey – or, at least, with cheese, cider and calvados!

Bearing witness to the prosperity of the land are some of the finest manor houses and farms in France – the typical half-timbered buildings known as *maisons à colombages*. The rich earth of the Auge lies on a bed of clay, and the buildings are constructed from this material, interwoven with beams of stained or painted wood. Most are beautifully maintained and are at their loveliest in springtime when they are perfectly complemented by apple orchards in full blossom.

This walk is set on the edge of this countryside, where the plain of

Falaise meets the high plateau of the Auge. This is cheese-making country, the cheeses all bearing the name of their place of manufacture. Livarot is just a few kilometres to the east, while to the south-east is Camembert, the village home of perhaps the most famous of cheeses. It is an attractive half-timbered village – with a museum – and well worth a visit in its own right.

St. Martin-de-Fresnay, where this walk starts, is a typical village of the Auge – a handful of farms and an assortment of half-timbered dwellings. From here, the route climbs quite steeply, with increasingly good views as you go. On reaching the top at the attractive village of le Billot, there is a well-placed picnic area from which to appreciate the panorama. Le Billot is reputed to have been at one time the most prosperous settlement in the area. After leaving the village, the way leads through lovely beech woods, particularly fine in the burning colours of autumn, and wanders up and down hills along a succession of *cavées*, the sunken, high-banked tracks so common in this locality. Half-timbered farms nestle into the slopes and the fields are grazed by black and white 'bespectacled' cattle. A short meander through the wide valley of the Oudon brings you home.

Cheese museum at Livarot

The Walk

1. From the cross-roads at St. Martin-le-Fresnay, head south-east on the D40 in the direction of le Billot. After crossing the River Oudon, take the first track on the left towards a half-timbered house. This track passes in front of the house and then climbs between high banks. The track then becomes wide and gravelled and you reach a wooden signpost at a track junction.

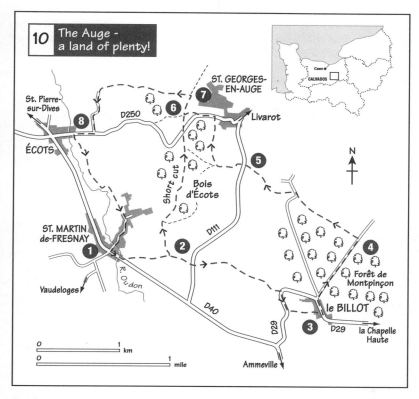

2. At this junction, you are meeting the Grande Randonnée du Pays. To take the short route, turn left here (S.P. to Bois d'Écots) and follow the yellow on red waymarking into and through the wood. The route is well marked all the way (there are two junctions, at each of which you bear left), and you will join the main walk again at Point 6.

For the main walk, continue ahead, in the direction of le Billot. The waymarks are again the yellow on red flashes of the Grande Randonnée du Pays. Passing a collection of very prosperous-looking half-timbered buildings, you reach a tarmacked road, where you cross straight over. The track now climbs uphill and you have good views behind. At the top you meet a tarmacked road on a hairpin bend, and you turn right down the road. Just before the road swings right, take a track on the left, which again climbs dramatically. At the top is a picnic site with magnificent views, and you have reached the village of le Billot. If you are not self-catering, continue along the path for just a few metres more (note the Foyer Rurale on your right) to where a fine half-timbered little auberge stands beside the road.

3. Turn left on the road beside the auberge, now leaving the GRP. At the fork at the edge of the village, bear right, and at the next fork, right again – now following blue waymarks and the signs to St. Georges-en-Auge. A long straight road takes you through the heart of the Forêt de Montpinçon.

4. When you reach the far side, a wooden signpost directs you to turn left to the Bois d'Écots and St. Georges, and you follow this track downhill along the edge of the wood. Where the track corners right, take a track on the left, which descends to meet another road. Turn right on the road, and after a few metres, left on a waymarked path skirting the wood. First bear right on this track and then continue ahead to come down to the D111.

5. Cross this road to a track that again begins to climb. Bearing round to the left, a sunken (and sometimes muddy) track leads you up to the wood. Now bear right on a clearly waymarked track (blue) through fine woodland. At the top of the hill you follow the waymarks, bearing left and then right to come out on the D250. Turn left on this road, and after about 100 metres, right on a track into the woods again. Shortly you arrive at an intersection of tracks where the Grande Randonnée du Pays crosses from left to right (yellow on red waymarks).

6. If you have taken the short cut you will arrive at this junction and continue straight ahead. If you have taken the main route, turn right here, following the yellow on red waymarks.

7. Reaching the first building on the left, take the track beside it, now waymarked in white. This sunken track soon goes steeply downhill. Where the track corners sharply left, look for a path (hidden!) going straight ahead downhill – the waymarks will confirm it. This track now descends with fine views on the right, and eventually comes out at a tarmacked road. Turn left on this and continue ahead to meet again the D250.

8. Here turn right in the direction of the village of Écots. Just before crossing the River Oudon, take a farm road on the left. If you look across the river before turning, you can see the humps and hollows of a medieval dwelling in the field opposite. Now continuing on the farm road, bear left around the farm and keep ahead on a broad grassy track with the river across the fields on the right. After 10 minutes or so, you arrive at a track junction and turn left. The waymarks lead you out to a road beside a farm, and you keep to this for about 15 minutes, passing a succession of interesting half-timbered buildings as you arrive in the village of St. Martin-de-Fresnay. Keep straight ahead to return to the cross-roads.

More Walks in the Area

The varied and gently undulating terrain of the Auge is prime walking country and is home to a multitude of waymarked circuits. For a selection of the most interesting walks in the region you could think of getting the Topoguide *Calvados – Pays d'Auge (Ref. 081)*. But there is also a series of more localised Topoguides published, each entitled *PR en Pays d'Auge*, followed by the region. The local one is *Pays d'Auge, de la Dives à la Vie*. All these are published in French only, but the maps are reproductions of sections of the IGN maps, and are easy to follow, particularly with the help of the waymarking.

If this wealth of publications leaves you baffled, opt instead for one of the free regional leaflets showing all the waymarked paths in the area – for the area around St. Martin-de-Fresnay, the leaflet has the grand title *Randonnée et Patrimoine de la Viette et de l'Oudon*. From this leaflet, you can work out a circular route for yourself – and the waymarking, as you found on this walk, is generally good. The leaflets are stocked by all Tourist Information Offices – locally, the office at Livarot can help you

One excellent short circuit in this leaflet (a route also described in the Topoguide *Le Calvados à pied (Ref. D014)*, and included as part of a longer ramble in the Topoguide *Calvados – Pays d'Auge*) is the 7km route starting from Vieux-Pont-en-Auge, just north of St. Martin. The 10th century church at Vieux-Pont is one of the oldest in Normandy, and from there, the route passes below the steep slopes of the Butte of Montarin before climbing it to gain a fine viewpoint above Castillon-en-Auge.

Another feature of the Auge region is the wealth of *haras* – horse-breeding stud-farms. The soil, grassland and climate of this region are apparently ideal for the rearing of thoroughbreds and trotters. Just a little farther north again from Vieux-Pont (near Lisieux), a pleasant 10km circuit starts from Les Monceaux – a place that also boasts a large stud-farm. From here the route climbs to give fine views of the verdant valleys around le Mesnil-Simon before descending again to the fields of elegant horses. The route is waymarked in yellow throughout – and is described in the Topoguide *Calvados – Pays d'Auge*.

The yellow on red waymarks you met on the described route indicate that it is part of a regional tour – in this case, the *Tour du Pays d'Auge*. If you would like to follow this Grande Randonnée du Pays farther, it heads north from St. Martin-le-Fresnay through Vieux-Pont (8km.) and on towards St. Julien-le-Faucon (a further 6km.) The route is clearly marked on the free leaflet mentioned earlier. Unless you have two cars handy, you will need the services of a taxi firm – the Office de Tourisme in Livarot should be able to help. To complete the Tour du Pays d'Auge, you would need a spare month or so! The route meets the north coast at Villers-sur-Mer and follows it to Honfleur, from where it returns south again passing near Lisieux and Livarot. A whole topoguide is devoted to the itinerary.

Places of interest nearby

You are in the region of two of Normandy's most famous cheeses – Camembert and Livarot. Camembert itself is a little village just south of Vimoutiers. It was here that a farmer's wife, Marie Harel, gave hiding to a priest during the Revolution, and in return he presented her with his secret recipe for cheese. The village now has an exhibition hall, the *Maison du Camembert*, and it is also possible to visit local farms still producing cheeses in the traditional way.

In Vimoutiers itself, the statue of Marie Harel in the main square was given by the employees of the biggest Camembert factory in the USA! The *Musée du Camembert* is in the Tourist Information Office, and here you can take a guided tour (in 5 languages), following the cheesemaking process from the arrival of the milk to the finished product – which, in high season, you will have the opportunity to sample. An odd extra is the large collection of cheese labels.

The cheese manufactured at Livarot, a few kilometres to the north, is a delicious pink-crusted affair. Again there is a museum relating to its production – this time in an old château in the town

Driving between Vimoutiers and Livarot , you pass through the curiously named village of St. Foy-de-Montgomery. Its name proved fateful, for it was here that Field-Marshal Rommel's convoy was hit by aircraft fire in July 1944. Suffering from head injuries, he never returned to the battlefield, but later took poison rather than be tried for his implication in the plot against Hitler.

The nearby town of St. Pierre-sur-Dives plays its part in the local industry by manufacturing the cheese-boxes. The roof of the vast medieval covered market hall was burnt down in 1944, but was carefully restored using no nails or screws, but only traditional chestnut pegs. The hall is purported to be the largest in France, but the market itself spills out of the doors and on to the surrounding land. Colourful, noisy and aromatic, it is said to be the most authentically traditional market in Normandy. The buildings of the nearby 11th century Benedictine abbey now house yet another cheese museum.

If after all that cheese hunting you are in need of a drink, it's time to pursue the cider trail. There are various caves and farms locally, but to the north, at Cambremer, begins *La Route du Cidre*, a well-marked trail of approximately 30km.. Traditional farms along this route produce not only cider, but also the spirit Calvados and the aperitif Pommeau (a delicious combination of the two). With many opportunities for tasting, it is up to you to decide how you are going to get yourself around – driving really cannot be recommended. Leaflets (in English) are available from any Office de Tourisme.

11. Beaumont-en-Auge, a town with a view

The hilltop town of Beaumont-en-Auge looks out over Deauville and the distant sea. On this walk you can enjoy those views and also many fine half-timbered buildings typical of the Auge region.

Grade: Easy

Distance: 6km (3¾ miles)

Time: 2 hours

Map: IGN Série Bleue 1712 O

Start and finish: The town square at Beaumont-en-Auge

How to get there: Beaumont-en-Auge lies about 6km west of Pont l'Eveque. In the town of Pont l'Evêque, follow signs to Caen (by the N175, not the autoroute). Before leaving the town, turn right on the D118, sign-posted to Beaumont-en-Auge.

Refreshment: Beaumont-en-Auge has a variety of restaurants and cafés.

Notes: This short walk is on easy paths throughout, and, at least in summer, is quite suitable for trainers. There is no refreshment en route, so on a hot day, you might like to carry fluid. And a pair of binoculars might be appreciated for the views.

Waymarking: The route follows the Grande Randonnée between points 1 and 3 and again between points 6 and 1 – the waymarks are white on red. Between points 3 and 6, the waymarking is yellow.

Introduction

Beaumont-en-Auge stands high on a spur of land 90m. above sea level. From the end of the town square, where the land drops suddenly, a viewing platform allows you to look out over the treetops to the valley of the River Touques – and Beaumont claims that no fewer than sixteen church spires can be counted somewhere below you. Where the Touques reaches the sea, the white buildings of fashionable Deauville and Trouville can be seen sprawling on its banks, and between them the bright azure of the channel is often crossed by ferries on their way to Le Havre.

In the same square stands a statue of Beaumont's most famous son, Pierre Simon Laplace. In 1749 he was born into a humble farming family and somehow went on to gain a place in the military academy in the town. Distinguished mathematician, physicist and astronomer, he rose to be president of the French academy and was given the title Marquis de Laplace. Now his statue looks out on a most pleasant tree-lined square, surrounded by fine half-timbered buildings with the colourful tables and brollies of an open-air restaurant spilling along one side.

A restaurant in the square

Beaumont was always a place of prosperity – ever since a Benedictine priory was first founded here by William the Conqueror in 1060. The priory survived until the Revolution, after which the military academy took its place. The affluence of Beaumont is still apparent, with various art galleries, craft shops and restaurants of high quality in its pleasant streets.

The walk taken here is a very easy one, winding through the woods and lanes behind Beaumont. The high ground permits frequent views of the distant sea, and there are also views of Beaumont itself, its distinctive church spire rising from the top of the hill. Interest is added by the quality and variety of fine half-timbered dwellings passed en route. And when you return, if the stylish restaurants are not for you, enjoy a picnic with a view on the benches at the end of the square, and finish the day with a short drive to elegant Deauville.

The Walk

1. From the square, turn left on the road towards Pont l'Evêque. In front of the school, turn right on the Chemin du Moulin, following the white on red waymarks. After passing the cemetery, the road forks and you keep to the left. After crossing the stream, the route climbs again and soon a road comes in on your right. Immediately afterwards, at a sort of cross-roads, follow the GR waymarks to the right.

2. After just a few metres, at a fork, bear left on the Chemin du Bois Jourdain. This hollowed-out track climbs quite steeply, giving good views into the valley behind. Reaching the top of the hill, just before the first houses, the track forks.

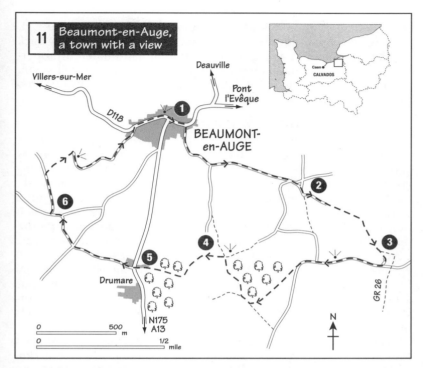

11 Beaumont-en-Auge, a town with a view

Villers-sur-Mer

Deauville

Pont l'Evêque

D118

BEAUMONT-en-AUGE

Caen • CALVADOS

1

2

3

6

4

5

Drumare

GR 26

N175 A13

N

0   500 m

0   1/2 mile

3. At this point the Grande Randonnée goes off to the left, but you keep right, now following yellow waymarks. Soon a road is reached. Turn right along this road and enjoy the distant views as you go. Where the road swings left, continue straight ahead on a pleasant track skirting the woods. On reaching a house at the end of the track, turn right on a sunken path with high banks. Still in the woodland, in about 25 metres, again bear right, continuing downhill. In springtime the banks in this wood are white with delicate wood anemones.

4. At the track junction at the bottom of the hill turn left on the broad stony track. There are good views of Beaumont across the fields. The track swings round and enters woods again, finally climbing to reach a main road.

5. Cross straight over here, still following yellow waymarks. After a few minutes walking, you arrive at a second intersection, and again go straight ahead. A few minutes farther on, at another junction, ignore the road on the right, and continue just a few metres more to another junction in front of a house. Here turn right on the Chemin de Bretocq.

6. After about 250 metres on this road, take a sunken track heading steeply downhill on the right, again picking up the waymarks of

the Grande Randonnée. At the bottom of the hill, continue ahead, now on a broad stony track. This track leads you all the way back into Beaumont, passing some interesting half-timbered proper- ties, and affording some good views of the town on its hill as you approach. At the junction with the main road, turn right and climb uphill to return to the square.

More Walks in the Area

For more walks in the immediate area, the Office de Tourisme at Pont l'Evêque can offer you a folder of 12 walks entitled *Randonnées autour de Pont l'Evêque*. But if the distant views of the sea are calling you to investigate at closer quarters, consider taking the coastal path, the GR 223, between Trouville and Honfleur – a distance of around 20km along a coast known as la Corniche Normande. On the way you pass through the Bois de Breuil, woodland resplendent with rhodo- dendrons in summer, and enjoy some wonderful views along a coast busy with shipping. The Grande Randonnée, as always, is well waymarked, but to assist with navigation, equip yourself with the IGN Série Bleue map 1711 O, on which the route is shown. A regular bus service runs between Trouville and Honfleur for the return (or out- ward) journey – ask at the Office de Tourisme in either town for details of times.

The Grande Randonnée running through Beaumont-en-Auge is the GR 26. Following this in a south-easterly direction for about 7km will bring you to the village of St. Hymer with its attractive old priory. To follow this GR, you would need the IGN map 1712 O. But if you arrive by car, a short circular walk of 8km is described from St. Hymer – it is one of the 12 routes in the *Randonnées autour de Pont l'Evêque* folder. Being well waymarked, it is easy to follow from the map alone, without the necessity of referring to the text, and makes a pleasant excursion into this wooded and quite hilly countryside.

Down at the sea again, the best walking Deauville has to offer is the long promenade along the boardwalk known as *Les Planches* – not exactly an expedition for walking boots! But the Office de Tourisme at Trouville (beside the harbour) can offer you a map showing two walks, both around 10km in length, and both with excellent sea views from the high ground east of the town.

And finally, if you visit Honfleur, call in at the Tourist Office (near the harbour) for their folder of 10 walks entitled *Randonnées autour d'Honfleur*. The 10km circuit in the valley of the River Orange is a pleasant route encompassing several attractive villages. It also includes part of a supposed 'Roman Road', once used to transport oysters and mussels from the coast inland. And for a coastal walk with a difference, try the ramble on the Marais de Pennedepie for a real breath of ozone.

Places of interest nearby

Down at Deauville there is lots to see, even if you do feel a little out of place in your walking gear. Deauville is for the famous, the rich and the aristocratic and you can see them all as you stroll the length of the sea-front on *Les Planches*. Sumptuous hotels and the shining white casino dominate the scene, looking out over the well-groomed sand and white-flecked ocean. Across the bridge, Trouville is less fashion-conscious, but more genuine. Trouville was here first with all the attractions – Deauville is a 20th century copy with an enhanced glitzy image that at least drew the casino trade. But Trouville is still the place to eat – and the place to browse, with its twice weekly market on the quay and tangy aromas arising from its permanent fish market.

From Trouville, if you have not the time to take the walk to Honfleur, at least take the drive along the corniche. In Honfleur, everything centres around the *Vieux Bassin* – the famous and very picturesque Old Dock, much beloved by the impressionists who gathered here in the 19th century. But there is much more of interest in the town. The Office de Tourisme can provide you with a 'Town Trail' of about 6km (also contained in *Randonnées autour de Honfleur*), touring the old streets and climbing to the Côte de Grâce and Mont Joli, with splendid views over the estuary of the Seine and the soaring Pont de Normandie.

Gastronomes would not want to miss the famous Pont l'Evêque cheese – the town is only 6km from Beaumont. The product is apparently at its best in early summer – but, be warned, it should be eaten on the spot and not carried home as a present. And if you want something with which to wash it down, visit the Coeur de Lion distillery on the N177 to the north of the town, where you can sample – and buy – cider, pommeau and calvados.

12. The Suisse-Normande – Climbing the Pain de Sucre

This is one of the classic walks of the region. The rocky outcrop known as the Pain de Sucre – or Sugarloaf – towers high above the River Orne giving some splendid views from its summit. And there are plenty more of those later on this walk, too.

Grade: Moderate – with a steepish climb just before the summit.

Distance: 7.5km (4¾ miles). A possible short cut can more than halve the distance – but you will miss a lot!

Time: 2½ hours

Map: IGN Série Bleue 1514 E

Start and finish: The church at le Vey, near Clécy

How to get there: Clécy is just south of Thury-Harcourt, on the D 562 between Flers and Caen. From Clécy, cross the river bridge to le Vey and continue ahead under the railway and up the hill to the church. There is a little space for parking in front of the church.

Refreshment: Attractive restaurants and bars line the river in le Vey and there are plenty more in Clécy. There is a pleasant little crêperie at St. Omer, about 10 minutes off the route.

Notes: Although there are some steep climbs and descents on this walk, the paths are well-defined and there is no reason why trainers should not be suitable in summer. Carry water on a hot day, and think of protection from the sun, as much of the route is exposed. Take the path across the Rochers de la Houle at your peril – it cannot possibly be recommended for children, even though it appears on a local walking leaflet! An alternative is described. And take your binoculars with you for all those views.

Waymarking: The route is marked by yellow flashes, except when following a Grande Randonnée, where the waymarking is white on red.

Introduction

The valley of the Orne in the heart of Normandy was casually dubbed the Suisse Normande by a visiting Minister of Tourism way back in 1932 – and the name has stuck. Maybe he had never even been to Switzerland. There are no lakes here and not a mountain in sight. Instead there are high rocky escarpments much beloved of rock climbers and paragliders, and for walkers there are wooded slopes to climb with fine views over the meandering River Orne way below. This may not be quite Switzerland, but it is certainly dramatic country-side by Normandy's standards.

Clécy is the 'capital' of the Suisse Normande, an attractive flower-decked stone town popular with tourists. Its twin across the

Picnic table with a view on the 'Route des Crêtes'

river is the little village of le Vey with riverside restaurants and camping. Of the river between a story is told, but you will need to be an out-of-season walker to check it out. One Christmas many years ago, thieves stole the church bell at Pont d'Ouilly. They galloped off downstream to Clécy where on a steep slope the horse stumbled and plunged into the river below. The bell clanged loudly as it fell and the robbers fled. Beneath the waters of the Orne the bell still lies concealed, and it is said that it can be heard tolling every Christmas Eve, summoning the faithful to Mass.

From le Vey it takes only half an hour to walk up to the Pain de Sucre, which is not really a hill, but a high point on the wooded rock face above the Orne. The summit is a ledge among the gorse and boulders, from where you have a bird's eye view of Clécy and of the silvery river cutting through the patchwork fields of the valley. On one side are the jagged outcrops of the Rochers de la Houle, rocks whose harsh faces are softened in spring by the yellow of gorse and broom. A path picks its way across them – and it is waymarked. You have an option to continue that way – but unless you have a head for heights, nerves of steel and thick gloves for clinging to the gorse bushes, don't even think of it! The more sober choice follows the length of the 'Route des Crêtes', a narrow road along the top of the ridge from which there are more magnificent views and picnic tables where you can sit and enjoy them. The descent towards the river is steep, but before you return there is another rocky ridge to cross. The Rochers des Parcs is a well-known rock climbing site with a classic view of the viaduct over the Orne, a scene much-painted by local impressionists.

The Walk

1. Keeping the church on your right, walk up the road, which climbs steeply uphill. In about 200 metres, take a path on the left, signed to the Pain de Sucre. You are following the GR 36 with white on red waymarks. The path soon enters woodland and climbs steadily with magnificent views. After about half an hour's walking, a sudden steep climb heralds your arrival at the summit (171 m.). The valley of the Orne is spread out before you and across it the hills rise some 80 metres higher, to a green peak prosaically known as l'Éminence.

2. When you are ready to move on, retrace your steps down the steep slope for about 20m. At the path junction, turn left downhill, and then continue ahead uphill (ignore a path going down on the left). There seem to be many waymarks nailed to trees here – just for the moment you are following yellow bars. Where the uphill slope is particularly steep, a tree in your path indicates a junction. If you are feeling particularly heroic, you can turn right here and follow the narrow yellow-bar-waymarked path across the Rochers de la Houle. For the recommended route, continue uphill to the road (5 minutes) and turn right along it. At the fork in the road, keep to the right and walk on along the Route des Crêtes with its superb views. A few more minutes walking will bring you to a *Pointe de Vue* – a clearing with picnic tables adjacent to a paragliding launch. The path across the Rochers de la Houle comes out to this point also. Now continue along the road, passing a hang-glider launching site, to where, opposite a low summit, a broad track heads off downhill on the right – a steep and rapid short cut to le Vey.

3. To continue with the main walk, keep ahead on the road to a sharp left hand bend. If you are drawn by the thought of the crêperie at St. Omer, continue around this bend into the village and turn left – a walk of 10 minutes or so. But to carry on with the walk, take the track on the right going downhill. This brings you to a farmhouse on a hairpin bend, where the track becomes a tarmacked road. The road descends very steeply to a fork beside a stone house. Here take the left hand track continuing around the hill. In about 200 metres, ignore a track climbing on the left and keep ahead to reach the farm buildings at le Haut du Vey.

4. Coming down to the road (D 133), turn left, and in a further 50 metres or so, branch right on a road sign-posted to the Rochers des Parcs. The road dips and then climbs again to a picnic site on a corner. Here you join the Grande Randonnée and follow the sign-posted direction *GR 36 Thury-Harcourt* along the road.

5. In about 50 metres, take a track on the right into the trees. The

path follows a rocky ridge above the Rochers des Parcs and there are fine views of the Orne viaduct and way behind it, l'Éminence. The path is lined with gorse and broom, a riot of colour in springtime. Eventually the way descends and passes under the railway to reach a road. Here turn right, and passing the Moulin du Vey, you come to a T-junction. Turn right and again cross under the railway to return to the church.

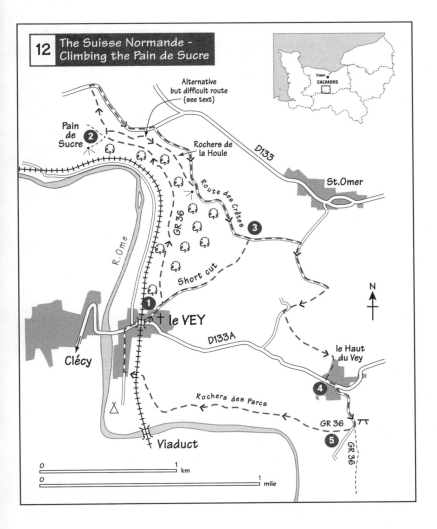

12 The Suisse Normande -
Climbing the Pain de Sucre

Caen
CALVADOS

Alternative
but difficult route
(see text)

Pain
de
Sucre ❷

Rochers de
la Houle

D133

St.Omer

Route des Crêtes

R.Orne

GR 36

❸

Short cut

❶

† le VEY

D133A

N

le Haut
du Vey

❹

Rochers des Parcs

GR 36

❺ GR 36

Clécy

† Viaduct

0   1
                     km

0   1
                                        mile

More Walks in the Area

The Suisse Normande is reputed to be the best walking country in Normandy – if you have worked your way through this book you will be able to judge for yourself. The GR 36 wends its way from Putanges in the south to Thury-Harcourt in the north, and there are in addition many waymarked circular walks. Oddly, it is difficult to get an overall view of the Suisse Normande. Two *départements* are involved, Calvados in the north down to Pont d'Ouilly, and in the south, Orne. Since each of these stocks their Offices de Tourisme with only their own walking literature, you will need to visit two centres to acquire a representative selection of walks.

The Pain de Sucre is in the north, for which the best Tourist Information is at Clécy, just across the river. Here you will find a folder of 15 walks entitled *Randonnées en Suisse Normande* (Suisse Normande here means the Calvados part – they are choosing to ignore Orne).. The maps in this folder are excellent and the waymarking on the ground is very good – you should have no difficulty following any of these routes without reference to the French text. At Thury-Harcourt, there is a short circuit of 6.5km following the high ground and cliffs above the loop of the river known as the *Boucle du Hom*. Weaving in and out of woodland with some excellent views and picturesque villages, this is quite an energetic but very pleasant half-day walk. For yet another *sportif* walk from this collection, the 10km route starting from the village of Croissilles, north of Thury-Harcourt, is interesting. At first following the GR 36 above the east bank of the Orne, there are fine viewpoints (and one or two steep climbs) before the route turns away to pass through the Parc de Croisilles. The leaflet curiously tells you what toxic plants you can find en route! And finally, for something different from this folder of walks, head north to the Forest of Grimbosq, where there are various waymarked circular walks, a fitness course and the GR 36 passing through – not to mention an animal park, ruins of a feudal château, an arboretum and more.

And crossing the border into Orne, try Walk 13 starting from the magnificent viewpoint at the Roche d'Oëtre. More routes in the south of the Suisse Normande are also suggested with this walk. For details of these and others, the Office de Tourisme at Athis de l'Orne is very well stocked and more than helpful.

Places of interest nearby

The Suisse Normande is country for outdoor enthusiasts. From Clécy, canoeing, mountain-biking, fishing and horse-riding are popular pursuits, while anyone with more ambitious ideas can go for rock-climbing or paragliding. And, of course, there's simply messing about on the river – in a pedalo or water bike hired from one of the establishments along the riverside.

For views, drive up to the orientation table behind St. Joseph's chapel off the D6 west of Thury-Harcourt, or take your picnic and head for the site at La Croix de la Faverie sign-posted from the centre of Clécy. Farther afield, there's the view from 365 m. Mont Pinçon in the west (near Campandre Valcongrain)– and in the south, do not miss the spectacle of the wild gorges below the Roche d'Oëtre (the starting point of Walk 13).

Thury-Harcourt, like so many of the towns in the Suisse Normande, was virtually destroyed in the fierce fighting of the Battle of Normandy. The Château was a casualty of the conflict, occupied by the Germans and set on fire as they fled. The ruins are a poignant reminder, but the grounds and formal gardens have been restored and the site is well worth a visit.

And should the day be wet, Clécy has thoughtfully provided for its visitors two worthwhile diversions away from the elements. The first is an exhibition of paintings by the local impressionist of last century, André Hardy – it's an attractive insight into the daily life of the time. The second is a truly superb model railway exhibition, the Musée du Chemin de Fer Miniature, said to be one of he largest of its kind in Europe. There are landscapes and towns representing many countries, with hundreds of buildings and vehicles not to mention the rolling stock. And if you're really not an enthusiast, you can always sit on the terrace (or in the cellar) with a glass of cider while everyone else plays trains!

The forest of Bellême (Walk 16)

Orne

13. Views from the Roche d'Oëtre

At the Roche d'Oëtre, a belvedere looks out over the deep wooded valley more than a hundred metres below. This short walk takes you down to a pretty village beside the river and climbs back through a forest of beech.

Grade: Moderate

Distance: 6km (3¾ miles)

Time: 2 hours

Map: IGN Série Bleue 1514 E

Start and finish: Parking at the Roche d'Oëtre

How to get there: From Pont d'Ouilly head south on the D167 along the riverside. After 3km., turn right to reach the village of Rouvrou. Here, turn left where signed to the Roche d'Oëtre.

Refreshment: For many years there was a bar/restaurant on the site of the Roche d'Oëtre. Sadly, *la Tempête*, the severe storm of December 1999, caused massive damage. Perhaps it will be restored some day. Meanwhile, there is a pleasant bar/restaurant just off the route in the village of Rouvrou.

Notes: This walk is all on good tracks – nevertheless, don't forget that they can be muddy after rain and out-of-season and choose your footwear accordingly. The route takes you down into a valley – and the return climb, although not too severe, is sustained. The viewpoint on the Roche d'Oëtre is literally on the edge of a precipice. Take care!

Waymarking: The route into the valley follows the Grande Randonnée (GR 36) and so is waymarked in white on red. After that, the waymarking is yellow.

Introduction

The Roche d'Oëtre is one of the most spectacular viewpoints in the Suisse Normande. From a high outcrop of rock you can look out over the wild and densely forested river valley way below you. This is a remote place – there is neither road, nor footpath going through that valley, but deep in the trees is a winding river, this time not the Orne but its tributary the Rouvre.

Back at the Roche d'Oëtre, an orientation table points out distant features of the view, while if you make your way down the slope you can look back and see the profile of a human face in the escarpment below the belvedere. Midway up that rockface, and quite inaccessible, is a cave, famous as the one-time hiding place of the local counter-Revolutionaries, the Chouans of Normandy. It is said that their chief, the Marquis de Frotté, concealed himself there for months and was supplied with food by folk from the nearby villages. It seems a remote enough hideaway.

From the Roche d'Oëtre this walk takes you down to the hamlet of

La Plisse, where the church looks out along the length of the valley, and on to the attractive and curiously situated settlements of les Planches and Rouvrou. Between them the river has turned through an almost complete circle, a loop whose ends are separated by just a narrow ridge of rock. This is the place to play pooh-sticks! Drop your twig in at Rouvrou and it will turn up at les Planches half an hour later – while you calmly stroll over the hill between! For a good view of the loop you can divert to a viewpoint known as the Site de St Jean. The way home then lies through the beech forest clothing the steep outer banks of the meander – a forest particularly glorious in autumn, as indeed is this whole beautiful valley.

Orientation table on the Roche d'Oëtre

The Walk

1. Leaving the Roche d'Oëtre, walk downhill on the D 301 in the direction of Rouvrou. After about 300 m., where the road makes a sharp left-hand corner, take a broad track on the right, waymarked with both white on red and yellow flashes. At the first cross tracks (250 m.), turn to the right, and after a few minutes, at the fork beside the reservoir, bear left. Continue following the same waymarking all the way down to the village of St. Philbert-sur-Orne.

2. On reaching a tarmacked road in the village, immediately turn left A broad track leads you downhill all the way, and emerges at the chapel at la Plisse with its views down the valley. Cross in front of the chapel and bear left, still following the excellent waymarking.

The path overlooks the valley of the Rouvre and finally you descend into the attractive stone hamlet of Les Planches, where cattle and goats graze in the apple orchards beside the river. The path takes you over the river and swings right on the far side. Now follow between the houses to come up to a narrow tarmacked road. Here the GR leaves you and continues to the right past the camping site, but you turn left and climb the hill. At the top the road swings right and you come down to join the main road. The River Rouvre is in front of you across the fields – you have just walked over the ridge between the ends of the meander.

3.   Turn left on the road and follow it down to the river. If you want to visit the Site de St Jean with its views of the meander, do not cross the river but keep straight ahead, following the signs. Turn right after the cemetery to reach the viewpoint. Returning to the road, now cross the river and take the first road on the left (waymarked). This begins to climb once more, and continuing straight ahead, you reach an earth track again. Now you enter a fine beech forest, and always keeping straight ahead (ignore the yellow dots on the trees on the left at one point) you return to the cross-tracks passed at the beginning of the walk. This time cross straight over, and at the road turn left to return to the Roche d'Oëtre.

More Walks in the Area

The GR 36 makes its way along the length of the River Orne from its source near Falaise to the sea beyond Caen. In the typical manner of a GR, it twists and turns to visit every scenic attraction in range – and in the Suisse Normande it has a field day. Arriving in Putanges, it follows the hills on the south shore of the Lac de Rabodanges with fine views all the way. The sides of the valley become steeper as the river enters the wooded Gorges de Saint-Aubert, accessible only on foot. North of la Forêt-Auvray there is so much to see that the GR divides itself into two – the western branch heading up to the Roche d'Oëtre and the eastern one continuing through the gorges. At Pont des Vers the branches re-unite and the route heads north past Pont d'Ouilly into Calvados. Here the GR soon crosses the river and makes a triumphal entry into le Vey along the Rochers des Parcs (see Walk 12). Leaving via the Pain de Sucre there are more magnificent views on the way to Thury-Harcourt and the Forêt de Grimbosq. The section between Putanges and Thury-Harcourt is about 50km – an ideal two-day walk with a stop at Pont d'Ouilly overnight. Moreover all three towns are connected by bus so you have no problem getting back to your starting point. Any Office de Tourisme should be able to help you with bus times and accommodation if needed. You would need to equip your-selves with the relevant IGN maps. The route actually crosses four of the Série Bleue series, so it would be less expensive, as well as more

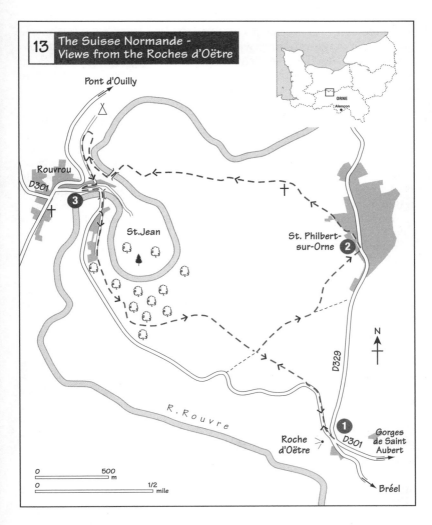

13 The Suisse Normande -
Views from the Roches d'Oëtre

Pont d'Ouilly

Rouvrou
D301
3

St.Jean

St. Philbert-
sur-Orne 2

N

D329

R . R o u v r e

Roche
d'Oëtre
D301 1

Gorges
de Saint
Aubert

Bréel

0   500
                    m
0   1/2
                    mile

informative, to get hold of the Topoguide *La Suisse Normande et le Pays de Falaise (Ref. 312)*

It is well worth walking through the wild Gorges de St. Aubert and a good starting point is the bridge at la Forêt Auvray. It is easy to follow the GR above the riverbank, but you would have to return by the same route as there is no crossing of the river. Farther up the valley, where the sides are perhaps less steep, there is an excellent circular walk of 9km starting beside the Lac de Rabodanges. This takes you into the upper end of the Gorges de St.-Aubert, but it is not for everyone as the ford crossing of the river requires some agility. The walk is entitled Les Gorges and is described in the folder *Val d'Orne – Petites Randonnées et Promenades.* The waymarking is good – you won't get lost in the gorge – but the route comes with an attached warning that you should respect the level of the river (check at the barrage E.D.F. at Rabodanges where it is controlled), have waterproof footwear and carry a first-aid kit.

Other walks in this collection present fewer problems, and the presentation of each is excellent with good sketch maps and points of interest clearly marked. One of the best circular routes follows the Grande Randonnée above the Lac de Rabodanges between Putanges and Ste.-Croix and returns on higher ground. There are many good views across the lake and countryside, and the route passes old manors and farmhouses, woods, streams, aged trees, lavoirs and much more – in all, 19 items are recommended for your attention.

Finally, there is a splendid educational walk, that could possibly be taken as an extension to the walk at the Roche d'Oëtre. The Maison de l'Eau et de la Rivière at Bréel has marked out a *Parcours Botanique*, a route of 10km across the hillsides between Bréel and the Roche d'Oëtre. More than 20 trees and shrubs are named along the path – a French and botany lesson combined. Details of the Parcours and an accompanying booklet can be obtained from the Maison de l'Eau et de la Rivière.

Places of interest nearby

South-west from the Roche d'Oëtre lie the attractive Gorges de Saint-Aubert (see More Walks section), and beyond them is the Lac de Rabodanges, created when the Orne was dammed to provide hydro-electric power. The lake is a popular location for fishing, canoeing and jet-skiing – and a cruise boat, the Val d'Orne, offers you the only opportunity to see the Orne valley from the water. Putanges-Pont-Écrepin is the regional centre, itself a pretty flower-decked town spanning the river.

The area around Putanges is delightfully rural and it seems every little village has a chapel, manor, château or medieval hall worthy of note. A leaflet, *Le Pays de Putanges*, will guide you around. Rabodanges has a 17th century castle that is home to a stud farm, while the old manor at Ste. Croix-sur-Orne is open to the public. In addition to its fine viewpoint over the Orne, La Forêt-Auvray has an old covered market hall and mill dating from the 15th century.

14. A woodland stroll at Bagnoles de l'Orne

At the heart of the Forest of Andaines, Bagnoles de l'Orne is a spa town and well worth a visit in itself. While there, you could take this very short walk in the forest, which includes a good viewpoint, an enormous ancient oak tree and the tiny chapel of St. Ortaire.

Grade: Easy

Distance: 9km (5½ miles)

Time: 3 hours

Map: IGN TOP 25 1516 ET

Start and finish: The Office de Tourisme at Bagnoles de l'Orne

How to get there: From the lakeside at Bagnoles, follow the direction of the D235 to La Ferté-Macé. The Office du Tourisme is on the left at the second roundabout, and there is parking alongside.

Refreshment: Bagnoles de l'Orne is well supplied with an assortment of restaurants and cafés.

Notes: This is an easy walk on good woodland tracks – in summer, trainers should be quite suitable footwear, but note that in winter or after heavy rain, the paths can be muddy. There is no refreshment en route, so carry fluids with you. Being almost entirely in woodland, this walk will offer good shade on a hot summer's day.

Waymarking: There are fine wooden signposts in the forest in addition to good coloured waymarking. The route of this walk is waymarked in yellow.

Introduction

Bagnoles de l'Orne owes all its prosperity to a horse. The story goes that, way back in the time of the Crusades, the Count of Tessé returned home from the battlefields with his charger, Rapide. But the horse had grown old and weary on his travels and was no longer living up to his name. Rather than kill him, as was the usual fate of such horses, the Count decided to set him loose in the forest. He was greatly surprised when, a short time afterwards, Rapide returned to his stable rejuvenated, strong and lively. Intrigued by what had happened, the Count decided to follow the horse's hoofprints back into the forest. The trail led to a warm stream gushing from the hillside – the stream now known as the Grande Source. The Count himself bathed in the water – and was likewise amazed at its effects. He apparently went off and fathered several children by the Dame de Bonvouloir and was so delighted with himself that he built the Tour de Bonvouloir (an observation tower in the forest) to show his gratitude. So was born the spa town of Bagnoles de l'Orne, now the largest spa in western France. 20,000 people a year come to benefit from these

Signpost in the forest

waters, which are acidic, mildly radioactive and constantly at a temperature of 24.5 C. The waters are said to be particularly good for circulatory disorders, including varicose veins, and for rheumatic problems.

Even if you are not seeking treatment, Bagnoles is an interesting town to visit. The atmosphere is still that of the 'Belle Époque' – the turn of the 20th century. The elegant white building of the casino overlooks a glassy lake and you can hire a horse-drawn carriage to take you on tour. Many fashionable residences and hotels are from the same period, as are the spa buildings themselves, couched under a steep hillside covered in parkland. Just as attractive is the stylish adjacent twin town of Tessé-la-Madeleine, where you can walk in the grounds of the 19th-century château to a rocky outcrop overlooking it all – thermal buildings, casino and lake are laid out before you.

From a walking point of view, Bagnoles is superbly situated – it is surrounded by the Forêt des Andaines, now part of the Parc Naturel Régional Normandie-Maine. This ancient oak and beech forest is criss-crossed by footpaths and there are many features of interest in its hidden depths. There is some claim that the forest is in fact Brocéliande, the setting for the tales of King Arthur and the Knights of the Round Table – although this is commonly accepted to be the Forest of Paimpont in Brittany. But the tales were written down by Chrétien de Troyes, a troubadour of the 12th century, when he was staying at the court of Eleanor of Aquitaine in nearby Domfront. Why would he have looked for a more distant forest in which to locate his stories?

Whatever the case, this is attractive woodland with fine vegetation and lots of wildlife including red and roe deer. The walk here simply leads you through the leafy glades to a high outcrop of rock known as the Rocher Broutin, from where there is a long view north across the agricultural plain towards La Ferté-Macé. On the way back you pass a huge oak around 400 years old and then arrive at the site of the tiny Chapel of St. Ortaire, which is the site of an annual pilgrimage in Easter week. Back in 580, St. Ortaire was a great healer and lived alone in the forest for 38 years. And returning to Bagnoles, spare a few minutes before leaving to visit the Roc au Chien and Capuchin's Leap – see below for the details!

The Walk

1. At the Office de Tourisme, face towards the Parcours Sportif in the forest behind. A wooden signpost points the direction of the *Sentiers de Randonnée* up the road to the left. Following this, you come to another wooden signpost naming the various circuits. For the first part of this walk you follow the *Circuit du Rocher Broutin*, and so head off on the broad track running beside the railway.

2. Coming up to the site of the chapel, turn left (away from the chapel) and cross under the railway to reach the road. Now turn right along the road and continue beside it around the bend. Just after the sign for the *Forêt des Andaines*, look for a track leading off on the right – there are yellow waymarks on the trees, but no other indication. The track climbs uphill through broom and bracken to reach a broader forest road, where you turn right and continue for about 150 metres.

3. Now turn left, again following a signpost to the Rocher Broutin. A few minutes walking along this track brings you to another broad forest road, where yellow waymarks invite you to turn left. After only about 30 metres, a sign points you to the right again and you continue through the forest.

4. Soon you arrive at another broad cross-track and are met by yet another fine wooden signpost. Turn left, and again almost immediately right, continuing under the trees before a very gentle climb to the Rocher Broutin. These attractive rocks are right at the forest edge with a view out over rural farmland. A bench has thoughtfully been placed for you to take in the view – and perhaps enjoy a picnic lunch. When you are ready to return, retrace your steps to the signpost at point 4, and this time, continue ahead in the direction of *Bagnoles de l'Orne via Chapelle de St. Ortaire*.

5. At the next junction, turn right (still signposted to Bagnoles) and follow beside the railway. At the first track junction, go straight over, but at the second, a junction with a tarmacked forest road, turn left and cross the railway. Where the road straightens out, a yellow-waymarked track on the right will take you directly back to

the chapel of St. Ortaire. But to see the enormous old oak tree, continue ahead on the straight road for about 400 metres.

6. Here a sign directs you to turn left to the *Chêne Hyppolite* – the oak tree is apparently named after a forester. The big old oak is in a clearing on the left at the bottom of the hill. When you have seen it, return to the road again (Point 6) and continue along it in the same direction for a further 30 metres or so. Now turn right, heading into the forest again on a broad track with yellow waymarks. Reaching a track junction, ignore the signpost directing you left to Bagnoles de l'Orne (this is now on a different circuit). Instead, turn right on a track which again bears yellow waymarks. On arriving at the chapel, go through the gate (this looks private, but isn't) and turn left to find yourself in front of the chapel and priory. The whole site is worthy of some exploration. When ready to leave, walk down the path to reach Point 2 again and continue ahead to Bagnoles.

More Walks in the Area

The Forêt des Andaines is part of the Parc Naturel Régional Normandie-Maine, a park whose headquarters is in an outbuilding of the Château de Carrouges, about 25 kilometres east of Bagnoles de l'Orne. The château is a magnificent building itself, but in the former chapter house you will find all manner of literature about the park. Several forests are included within its bounds (Écouves, Perseigne, Sillé and others as well as Andaines) and relating to each is a *Circuit de Découverte*, a route particularly describing flora and fauna. Maps of each forest are available showing footpaths and recommended routes. Booklets and folders of walks abound – but sadly, no Topoguide covering this area has yet been produced.

For information on the Forêt des Andaines, the Park Headquarters (and possibly Tourist Information at Bagnoles de l'Orne) can offer you a map with a dozen or so marked circuits. The lengths and times of each are to be found on the reverse of the map. A short commentary is also given – but it is not essential to understand it, as the waymarking of these routes is quite good enough in itself.

The GR 22 runs through Bagnoles and then on through the eastern part of the forest. The white on red waymarking is easy to follow, but the IGN Top 25 map mentioned above will give you a clearer idea of the route. After about 7km you come to the lake in the Vallée de la Cour where there is a bar/restaurant – you could park the car and start from here as an alternative. From the lake, you can follow the GR (now also accompanied by yellow waymarks) over the hill and down into the Gorges de Villiers. In an attractive remote site beside the River Gourbe is the tiny Chapel de St. Antoine with its *fontaine* and cross. A site of pilgrimage for many years, it was destroyed in the Revolution, but rebuilt again a century or so later. Sadly, it was also damaged by

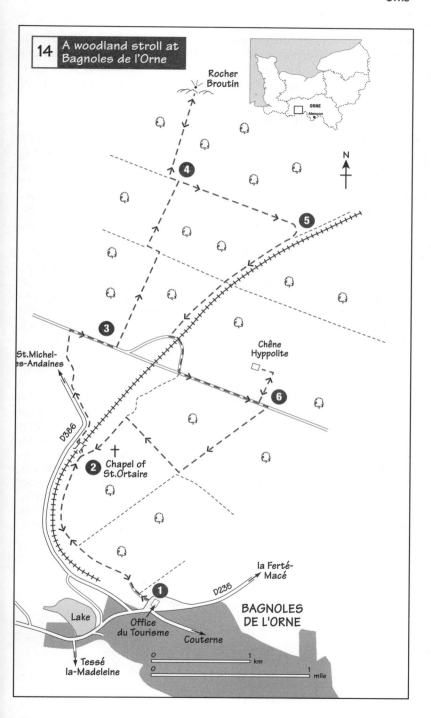

14 | A woodland stroll at Bagnoles de l'Orne

Rocher Broutin

ORNE
Alençon

N

St.Michel-es-Andaines

D386

Chêne Hyppolite

Chapel of St.Ortaire

la Ferté-Macé

D235

BAGNOLES DE L'ORNE

Lake

Office du Tourisme

Couterne

Tessé la-Madeleine

0   1 km
0   1 mile

the great storm just before the turn of this century, but hopefully will be restored to its former rural beauty. The route of this walk is marked on the forest map – the circuit from the lake is about 6km., taking the whole route from Bagnoles will add something like an extra 7km in each direction.

Places of interest nearby

Starting from the church in Tessé-la-Madeleine, you can take a walk (or a train ride in summer) through the grounds of a château that is now the Mairie to reach the viewpoint known as the Roc au Chien. Apparently a dog was once in the habit of eating young girls here! The grounds contain an arboretum with, among other fine specimens, several giant sequoias, but sadly *la Tempête* has taken its toll. From the viewpoint you look down on the spa buildings and across to the lovely parkland behind them.

'Capuchin's Leap' is directly above the spa buildings and can also be seen from the Roc au Chien – although it is certainly worth taking a look at closer quarters. Legend has it that in the early days of the discovery of the spa, a Capuchin monk came to the town to take the cure for his lameness. All went well and he demonstrated the miracle that had been wrought by leaping between the two pointed rocks high above the spring. To get the measure of this feat, take one of the paths into the attractive parkland behind and above the spa buildings.

Just south-west of Bagnoles, the village of Jouvigny-sous-Andaines is home to the Ferme du Cheval de Trait – a farm where you can watch displays of horse-drawn carriages and take a ride in one yourself. Not far away, at the edge of the forest, is the viewpoint Tour de Bonvouloir and the old Chapelle St. Geneviève where there is a picnic site. Other forest sites include a central lake (Maré aux Oies), popular with wildfowl and another high viewpoint at Mont-en-Gérôme.

6km north-east of Bagnoles is the town of La Ferté-Macé, renowned for a particular culinary delicacy, *tripes-en-brochettes* (skewered tripe!). If this appeals to you, take a few moments before or after your feast to look at the church with its unusual facade of coloured patterned stonework, and perhaps the Toy Museum, housed in what was once the municipal baths.

15. On the edge of the Forêt d'Écouves

The vast Forêt d'Écouves clothes the highest hills in Normandy and through it run many waymarked trails. This one is a little different, dipping in and out of the forest edge, and offering some good views along with a very pretty stretch beside a tumbling river.

Grade: Moderate

Distance: 10km (6¼ miles)

Time: 3 hours

Map: IGN TOP 25 1616 ET

Start and finish: The church at Livaie

How to get there: Livaie lies just north of the D2, about mid-way between Carrouges and Alençon

Refreshment: Simply – none! The nearest place of any size is Carrouges, about 12km to the north-west.

Notes: The terrain here is undulating and the route does include one or two steepish climbs. In the forest the tracks are generally good, although the path beside the stream requires a little agility. Walking boots would probably be the footwear of choice at any time of year, but you could probably get away with trainers in a dry summer. Food and water must be carried with you as there is none en route. And for those who run out of steam, it is possible to cut out the last 3km or so by following the main road home from Point 5.

Waymarking: The route is waymarked in yellow throughout

Introduction

The Forêt d'Écouves is the largest of the forests of southern Normandy and is included in the Parc Naturel Régional Normandie-Maine. Tracts of oak and beech, interspersed with newer stands of pine, stretch out over the rolling landscape as far as the eye can see – the forest covers 14,000 hectares! The heights here are part of the *Massif Armoricain*, a chain of hills formed far back in the Primary era, some 600 million years ago. The hard ancient rock can be seen projecting among heather and broom at a picturesque site known as the Rochers du Vignage. Among these hills is the highest point in Normandy – and indeed in western France – the Signal d'Écouves at 417 m. But the summit itself is clothed in dense forest – there are many better places for a view and you will pass one or two on this walk.

The forest is criss-crossed with tracks and there are many named intersections – the Croix de Médavy, Croix Madame, Carrefour du Chêne au Verdier and lots more. At several of these you can still find an old *borne* or wayside stone, engraved with the name of the ancient road through the forest. Most date from the 17th century – a time when the roads would have been particularly important for transporting

La Butte Chaumont

wood for the building of warships. Since then many forest industries have flourished, dependent on the easy availability of fuel, and in the 19th century provision for iron foundries and glassmaking denuded great tracts of woodland. By 1863, things had gone far enough, and a policy to replace the lost oak and beech with pines was begun. The forest is today both deciduous and coniferous, and part of its charm is this variation in its character.

Autumn sees the forest in its most attractive colours – and if you are interested in fungi, this is also the time to track down boletus and the delicious girolles among others. If you are in doubt about what you have found, it is to the local pharmacy that you should go for advice! Wildlife abounds in the forest at any time of year and you have a good chance of spotting deer (red and roe) – although the wild boar are nocturnal and therefore rather more elusive. Wildflowers, too, are abundant and a *Circuit de Découverte* starting from the Carrefour de Rendez-vous will tell you what to look out for.

The route chosen for this walk weaves in and out of the forest edge – and so provides a little contrast. Livaie, where the walk begins, is merely a tiny village that presumably flourished in the heyday of forest industry, but from here the route heads into interesting country. Following a track that was once used to take the wood to the iron forges at the village of la Roche Mabile, you climb to a rocky forest viewpoint known as the Pierre au Chat. Dipping down again and leaving the forest, there are more open views – ahead of you is a conical hill known as the Butte de Chaumont. Its shape suggests that this could have been a volcano some 500 million years ago. Although only 378 m in height, there is often a mist clinging to its summit – and be warned by the local adage 'When Chaumont wears his hat, man puts on his coat'! Before returning to Livaie there is a delightful section following a babbling stream as it tumbles over rocks deep in the forest – and those with enough energy can climb yet another hill with a view before they go home.

The Walk

1. With the church behind you, turn left and walk down to the road junction. Here turn right, and continue downhill to the cross-roads on the main road. Turn right and walk on the verge alongside the main road for about 350 metres, to where a sign directs you left to the village of la Blottière. Now you walk downhill (enjoy it while you can!) to reach a cross-roads at the bottom where you turn left. The road begins to climb and becomes a rough track – this is the Chemin des Charbonniers, once used to transport wood to the forges of la Roche Mabile. Continue climbing on this broad waymarked track to the top of the hill.

2. At the top of the hill is a cross-roads, where taking the path to the right brings you in a few minutes to the rocky viewpoint called the Pierre au Chat. It is a private path but you are welcome to follow it – except on Thursdays and Sundays, when it is closed for hunting. Returning from the viewpoint to the cross-roads, turn right (i.e. maintain your original direction) and continue downhill on a track that becomes quite sunken between banks. A first cross-tracks is passed where the yellow waymarking clearly indicates the path ahead, but at the second junction with a major track, you are directed to turn left leaving the wood.

3. On reaching the tarmacked road, turn right, and then in about 30 m. take the road to the left. Ahead of you at this junction is a fine view of the hump-backed Butte de Chaumont. Its summit affords a 360º panorama – the Romans had a camp up there and it was an observation post in the 1914-1918 war. Continue along the road for a few minutes to reach a road junction, where you turn left and head towards the forest again.

4. On reaching the forest edge, where the road corners sharply left, take a waymarked path on the left beside the banks of the Ruisseau de la Roche Élie. Walking upstream, you soon plunge into the depths of the forest. The rushing clear waters are pure enough for trout and crayfish and here you can look out for deer – or at least find their footprints in the damp earth beside the stream. After almost an hour following the meanders of this stream through the woodland, a lake appears on your left and shortly afterwards the path climbs to reach a broad track where you turn right. This track was the old Alençon – Carrouges road –

originally a Roman route. Now you climb the track to reach the D2, the present road between the two towns.

5. If you are tired at this point, you could always follow the D2 back to Livaie, which is now only about 1km away to the left. But to continue with the walk, cross straight over this road to a stony forest track opposite. The broad track heads away from Livaie and climbs steeply above the road, soon cornering to the left. Here you are briefly on a Grande Randonnée. In the straight stretch that follows the corner, look for a yellow waymarked track on the left, between tracts 324 and 327. The path climbs with conifers on the left and mostly deciduous forest on the right at first – but soon the pines take over completely. Ignore all side tracks and continue to the top of the hill. From here it is possible to see the church at Livaie away to the left (somewhat obscured by foliage in summer) before you begin the descent. The mosses and lichens on this north facing slope are quite prolific (and slippery) and the destruction caused by *la Tempête* is very evident. Eventually you come down to a wide forest road.

6. Turn left on this forest road (you can again see the white on red flashes of the Grande Randonnée) and continue downhill. After several minutes on this road, just after a left hand bend and before a right hand bend, a yellow waymarked track leads down into the forest on your right. Taking this, you quickly descend to a tarmacked road.

7. Turn right on this road, which runs above a small valley with a stream. At the fork in the road, bear left, and climb yet again to reach a cross-roads. Here turn left, and in 15 minutes or so, arrive in the village of Livaie.

More Walks in the Area

There are so many tracks in this forest – it is easy to park at a cross-roads and just head off on any one of them. Nevertheless this forest is vast and dense, and if you are not following a waymarked trail, you had better take a ball of string with you! Several cross-roads have display boards giving plans of circular routes, their distances and the colour of their waymarking. But if you want to plan things before you go, get hold of a little book called *Promenons-nous en Écouves*, available from the Park Headquarters at Carrouges. In this you will find 8 short walks (the longest is 5.5km.) in the most interesting parts of the forest. The maps in this book are stylised and very clear, so you won't get lost – but a degree of competence in French would help with the extensive text. Even so, using routes alone you can find your way to the Signal d'Écouves, the Rochers du Vignage, ancient oak trees, forest lakes and much more. Sadly, the book lacks an overall plan of the forest – you would do well to get the IGN Top 25 map mentioned above.

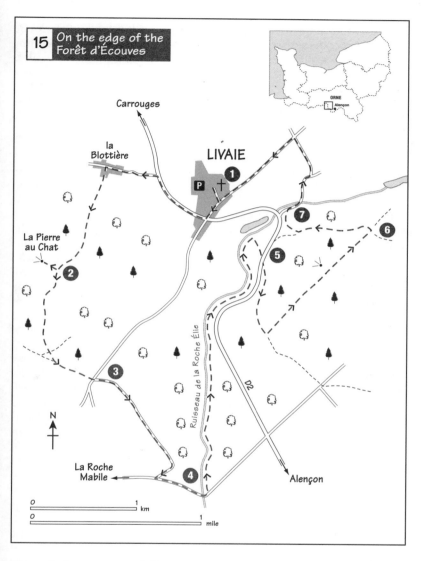

If you do have a copy of this IGN map, you can follow the routes of two Grandes Randonnées that pass through the forest – the GR 22 heading east-west and the GR 36 running north-south. You briefly met the GR 36 on this walk. Grandes Randonnées are always well waymarked, and it would be quite possible to follow either of these through the forest – but public transport doesn't help much here and there are no near towns for a taxi. Perhaps two cars is the only answer if you fancy a linear walk

If walking on the outskirts of the forest is more appealing, the Park headquarters at Carrouges stocks a folder of walks entitled *Balades de Bocage en Écouves,* with walks starting from several of the surrounding villages – the walk here is described in this collection. These leaflets are well-produced, with clear sketch maps and the waymarking on the ground is good. If you have some command of French it will add an extra dimension – but you should have no difficulty following the routes without. The short 7km circuit starting from Carrouges itself is easy and interesting – but there are plenty of other options.

Places of interest nearby

There is plenty of interest in the forest itself. At the Croix de Médavy in the north there is an American tank left by the French 2nd Armoured Division after they heroically evicted the German forces from the forest over two days in August 1944. There are good walks from the Croix Madame, a nature trail at the Carrefour de Rendez-Vous and a *Parcours Sportif* at the Carrefour du Chêne-au-Verdier. From this latter cross-roads, a path of about 1.5km will take you to the splendid Rochers de Vignage – the rocks can also be reached via a short path leading from the D 26, just south of its junction with the road to le Chêne-au-Verdier.

There are other forested hills in the south of Normandy – just a little to the south-west are the range with the rather grand name of Alpes Mancelles. The highest point here is the Mont des Avaloirs – at 417 m., the same height as the Signal d'Écouves. This time there is a view – an observation tower has been erected with an orientation table on the top platform. On a windy day it can be an exciting experience! The Alpes Mancelles region is well supplied with walking routes – and with mountain-bike trails if you care to take to two wheels instead. Details of these can again be obtained from the Park Headquarters at Carrouges. A little stone hamlet on the River Sarthe, St Céneri-le-Gérei, has been dubbed one of the prettiest villages in France – it is certainly popular with local artists. Four short walks have been described from here – but, on a personal note, our route failed since there was no longer a footbridge over the Sarthe. Perhaps it has now been re-instated.

And if you would like yet more forest, crossing the Normandy border into the Département of Sarthe will bring you to the Forest of Perseigne. This forest is again part of the Parc Naturel Régional Normandie-Maine – a good map is available and there is lots of potential for walking.

16. In the forest of Bellême

The hilltop town of Bellême stands on the edge of a beautiful forest of oak and beech. Here you follow the woodland trails to reach the Étang de la Herse, the lake at its heart, in whose dark waters the trees are seen to have perfect reflections.

Grade: Easy to Moderate

Distance: 10.5km (6½ miles)

Time: 3 hours

Map: IGN TOP 25 1817 OT

Start and finish: The Church of St. Sauveur, Place de la République, Bellême.

How to get there: Bellême sits in the south-eastern corner of Normandy, east of Alençon and Mamers on the D 955. The church is in the centre of the town and there is parking in the square beside it – except on market day (Thursday), when other places are available.

Refreshments: Bellême has a variety of restaurants, bars and cafés. En route there is a restaurant close to the Étang de la Herse and there is also a picnic table beside this lake.

Notes: This is a fairly gentle wander on well-marked forest tracks. Nevertheless, all forests can be muddy in winter and good footwear will be needed unless the weather has been particularly dry. The only climb of note is that back into the town. This is a pleasant walk on a hot day as it is almost entirely in the shade of the forest.

Waymarking: The route is waymarked in yellow throughout. It appears as Route no. 4 on a local leaflet – hence the occasional yellow 4 painted on trees etc.

Introduction

Bellême is the capital of the Perche, a rolling countryside of farms and patchwork fields, the original home of those superb heavy work horses, the Percherons. You aren't likely to see any Percherons on this walk in the forest, but just a few kilometres to the east is the Manoir de Courboyer where they graze in the fields and give displays of their strength to summer-time visitors.

Bellême is a town perched on a hill and below that hill the forest spreads north across the folded landscape as far as the eye can see. The Forest of Bêlleme is a remnant of the great forest that in Roman times covered all southern Normandy – and indeed three-quarters of France. Over the centuries, it has accommodated Roman camps and given shelter to hermits seeking solitude, seen the formation of religious orders and provided a living for the carpenter and the clog-maker. Now it is a carefully managed forest where the oak is supreme – the beeches are planted to give shade in the early years, thus ensuring a long knot-free trunk before the branches are formed.

At the end of the day (which is anything up to 200 years) the oak is used for everything from paper-making to furniture and veneer, depending on the quality of each individual tree.

Setting out from Bellême on its hilltop, the walk soon plunges into the silent dappled-light of this particularly beautiful forest. Generations of oaks and beeches line every path and between and among them are holly, holm oak, silver birch, spruce, Douglas fir and the rest. At one point the land rolls before you across a young plantation bright with gorse and heather. At length the path reaches the Étang de la Herse, a long oval lake where the beauty of the surrounding trees is faultlessly reproduced in the reflections. Regrettably the road through the forest passes close to this lake – although it fortunately can't be seen, only heard. Across the road from the lake is the mysterious Fontaine de la Herse, a spring surrounded by stones with Latin inscriptions. Nothing is known about its origins – there is a tale that it was first brought to light by Saint Martin de Tours ploughing the land in the 4th century. Restored by the local landowner in 1770, a doctor then declared its iron-rich waters to be good for just about every affliction. The Boule d'Or auberge in Bellême, thrived on the many 'curistes' who came to take the waters – a constant supply was carried from the *fontaine* in panniers on the backs of donkeys. But Bellême's heyday as a spa was short lived. Now the waters are no longer orange – although the surrounding blocks certainly are. Looking carefully, you can still see Latin inscriptions invoking Aphrodite, Mars, Mercury and Venus. A latter-day caption reads 'Eau non Potable'.

On the way home, the walk follows the route of an old railway line through a deep cutting and dives again into the oak and beech forest alongside a Parcours Sportif. Once back in Bellême, it is worth taking a few more moments to explore the interesting town before you leave. The arch into the Place de la Republique is the only remnant of the old ramparts, but the Rue Ville-Close (through the archway) is famous for its well-preserved 17th- and 18th-century classical houses. And finally, mention should be made of the fungi. Every September the world's mycological specialists descend on this little town for their annual conference in which the general public is invited to share. Consequently, shops and Office du Tourisme sport a wealth of fungi literature. Autumn is the time to find fungi in the forest – and if you want to know if they're edible, the chemist is the source of authority!

The Walk

1. From the church, walk uphill through the square towards the arch. Do not go through it, but instead turn left and go down some steps – a board tells you that this is the start of the *Promenade la Herse*. Now continue downhill between the old buildings on the Rue de la Herse. At the bottom you reach le Clos Fleuri, a house that was once a railway station. Here turn right and follow the track of the

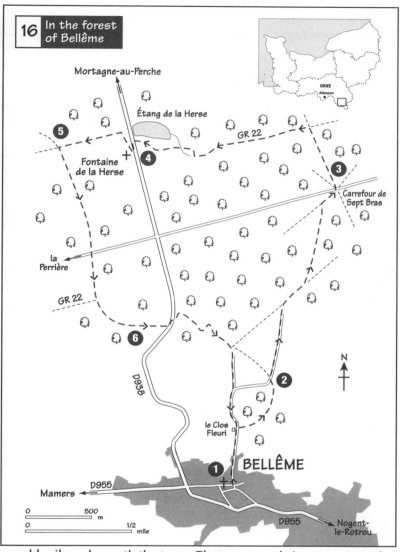

old railway beneath the trees. There are good views across to the forest.

2. Coming out to a tarmacked road with a house opposite, turn right and pass the entrance to the Centre de Vacances as you head towards the forest. The tarmacked road becomes rough and stony as you go. In the forest, keep to the main track uphill, following the yellow waymarks. Soon the track on the right is marked with a yellow 2 – No. 2 route leaves you here, but you continue on the

main track and will follow Route no. 4 all the way. A board with an oak leaf logo points out a *Vieille Futaie de Chêne Rouvre* – an Old Plantation of Sessile Oaks. This is one of the boards of the Circuit de Découverte – if you are interested in a diversion, its length is a mere 2km and the green boards are easy to follow. But the main route continues up the broad track, which is joined by another from the left to reach the junction known as Carrefour de Sept Bras (except that there is also a sign calling it Carrefour de la Reine Blanche!).

3. At this junction, cross over the tarmacked road, and bearing slightly left, walk downhill on the Route Forestière du Château, in the direction of Éperrais. At the bottom of the hill, turn left and take the path between plots 29 and 30, now following the waymarking of Grande Randonnée 22, which crosses the forest. The path dips down and climbs again, now crossing the open heath of a young plantation. Pines and silver birch lead you down into another valley. On re-entering the denser forest the path makes a sudden left turn and descends to two wooden bridges. Ahead is the beautiful Étang de la Herse with an inviting picnic table beside the water.

4. Continue along the side of the lake (water on your right) to reach steps climbing up to the road. Cross the road directly (with care) and walk uphill to the left for a few metres before turning right to find the *fontaine* with its curious inscription and a board to tell you all about it. From here, turn right and, still following the white on red waymarks of the GR, find a track on which you turn left to go back into the forest. After 5 minutes or so of walking, the VTT track goes off on the right, but you continue ahead. A further few minutes on, at the top of a little rise, you reach a 4-way track junction.

5. At this junction, turn left and continue to follow the waymarks of the GR. This track is now the route of an old railway and after 20 minutes or so you cross under a road bridge. The trees tower above the banks on either side. As the track begins to curve, the GR leaves you and turns right, but you keep to the railway track around the curve and on to meet the main road again.

6. At the road turn left uphill to a parking area on the opposite side. Near the top of this lay-by, a path on the right leads in to a *Parcours Sportif* in the forest. Keep to this Parcours as far as no. 6, a pull-up bar, after which the route (now waymarked in yellow) turns right, downhill. Following the waymarks, you arrive at the forest edge and walk across rough ground to reach a stony road beside a house. Here Bellême can be seen on the hill in front of you, and you go straight ahead at every junction (passing again le Clos Fleuri) to return to the church on the hilltop.

Walking back to Bellême

More Walks in the Area

The friendly little Office de Tourisme in Bellême is a splendid place to browse. It is packed with literature of all kinds, and among them an excellent series of inexpensive walking leaflets. It seems that each commune (or group of small communes) in the Perche has devised a number of waymarked circuits in its surrounding area. The required maps are contained in the leaflet (along with some interesting text, but it's not essential to understand it). On the ground the waymarking is first-class. The route you have just taken is one in the Bellême leaflet – and was specially recommended for this book by the Office du Tourisme.

Another recommended walk is one at La Perrière, 10km away at the western end of the forest. A route of 12.5km takes you to visit an aged oak deep in the forest. On the way to find it you pass an old 14th century château and the remains of a Roman camp. The oak, known as the Chêne d'École, is thought to be more than 300 years old – a young tree when Louis XIV was on the throne. Standing 40 metres high with a straight trunk free of branches, it is a role model for all the oaks of the forest. La Perrière itself is worth a look around – it is a town of remarkable old stone buildings and there is a splendid view from the church across the rolling fields and forests of the Perche. A further short circuit of 3km (described on the leaflet) takes you on an interesting tour – and there is another small leaflet (in French) telling you about each building in great detail.

Back at Bellême, there are other described routes in the forest. But for something a little different, take the 9.5km circuit *La Croix Feue*

Reine which takes you to a hill outside the town from which the siege of Bellême was conducted by Blanche de Castile in 1229.

Places of interest nearby

The Manoir de Courboyer has already been mentioned as a place where you can find Percherons. The 15th- to 16th-century manor is just north of Nocé, about 8km east of Bellême, and is open all day in July and August and at weekends in September and October. In addition to the magnificent horses, you can take a guided tour round the manor and enjoy an exhibition on the history of the Perche from prehistoric times to today.

The original capital of the Perche was the bigger town of Mortagne, 17km to the north of Bellême. It too sits on a hill with views over the surrounding countryside. The 16th-century church and the *hôpital* from the same era are worth a visit. If you feel like exploring a little more, go on to the north-east to the Forêt de la Perche. Here amid the oaks and beeches you will find several pools along the line of the River Avre, some offering facilities for boating and bathing. On the western edge of this forest is the Abbaye de la Trappe, the original home of the Trappist monks who observe a strict rule of silence. The abbey itself can't be visited, but there is a shop selling produce from abbeys all over Normandy.

The little town of La Perrière is mentioned in the More Walks section. Even if you don't take the forest walk there, do have a look at the town with its interesting buildings. It seems that every village and town in the Perche has an old church, manor or château of some note. By no means all are open to the public, but this is a country in which to just to browse and look – and any Office de Tourisme can offer you leaflets to guide your steps.

The River Seine at Les Andelys (Walk 20)

Eure

17. The Abbey of le Bec-Hellouin

The ancient abbey at le Bec-Hellouin was once one of the great schools of Christianity in Europe. Arrive at this sacred place as the penitents of old must have done – on foot through the forest.

Grade: Moderate

Distance: 22km (13¾ miles)

Time: 6 hours

Map: The route covers two maps – IGN Série Bleue 1812 O and 1912 O. But this classic route can also be found on two free leaflets (*Vallées de Risle et de la Charentonne,* from the series *L'Eure au rythme des Vallées* and *Bienvenue autour de la Risle Brionnaise)* and in the Topoguide *L'Eure à pied.*

Start and finish: The central cross-roads at Brionne

How to get there: Brionne stands on the River Risle, south of the Brotonne Regional Park. At the centre of the town is a cross-roads (on the west side of the river). There is some parking next to the cross-roads and more at the Office du Tourisme on the Rue Géneral de Gaulle (from the cross-roads, head away from the river and *donjon*).

Refreshment: Brionne has an assortment of bars and restaurants. En route, there is a handful of pleasant eating houses at le Bec-Hellouin, a couple of bar/cafes at Pont-Authou and another beside the road at Livet-sur-Authou.

Notes: This longish walk is entirely on good tracks and minor roads. It does involve a measure of ascending and descending as it crosses three river valleys. No short cut is possible as Pont-Authou is the only crossing of the River Risle – so be sure you can manage the distance, or simply return directly from le Bec Hellouin. You could carry food and drink with you, but there is plenty of opportunity for resuscitation en route.

Waymarking: The route is almost entirely on Grande Randonnée (waymarked in white on red) with just a short section around Pont-Authou waymarked in yellow.

Introduction

In 1034, Herluin was a knight at the court of the Count of Brionne when he made the sudden decision to forsake his former existence and devote his life to God. Swapping his charger for a humble donkey, he set off into the forest. He stopped beside the brook or bec – a word deriving from the Norse, as is 'beck' in northern England. Nine others immediately joined him. Seven years later the number was 34 – and so was founded the Abbey of le Bec Hellouin.

The following year, a visitor from Italy came to the settlement – Lanfranc, a cleric and scholar who had been teaching at Avranches. He stayed, became abbot and developed a school of theology at the

The River Risle at Brionne

abbey. He also became the friend and advisor of William the Conqueror. One of his pupils went on to become Pope Alexander II – and he then made Lanfranc Archbishop of Canterbury, Primate of all England. Lanfranc was just the first of a long line of senior clergy in the English church to have spent time at le Bec Hellouin. After his death, his archbishopric passed to Anselm, Italian theologian and philosopher, who again had been abbot of le Bec Hellouin. Look at the plaque on the wall of the St. Nicolas tower to find the names of many others who followed to England. The abbey still has links with Canterbury as it has with the University of Cambridge.

Le Bec Hellouin continued as an intellectual centre, and in the 17th century came under the Maurists who developed it further. As with most others of it kind, fell victim to the Revolution. It was pillaged, used as a prison and allowed to fall into disrepair. In 1948 the Benedictines came back to take over the ruins, restore them and create a viable community. The monks make money for these enterprises by producing and selling pottery – there is a shop in the abbey. They also welcome visitors on frequent guided tours.

The walk here starts 6km away in the town of Brionne. It was here that Lanfranc first met William the Conqueror – who was besieging the place at the time. The old *donjon* (keep) on its hill above the town is a survivor of that siege. After a tour around the *donjon*, the walk sets off through the forest. This is undoubtedly the way to approach le Bec-Hellouin – you may hear its bell tolling before you catch the first glimpse of the abbey through the trees. Outside the abbey, the village of le Bec- Hellouin is picturesque in true Normandy fashion, its streets lined with well-kept half-timbered houses garlanded with flowers. You could easily pass an afternoon here – as well as the abbey, there is a little museum of mechanical instruments, and the restaurant opposite the abbey gates, with its colourful tables spilling on to the pavement, looks an interesting enough diversion. You could always choose to return directly to Brionne.

The full route will take you another 4 hours from here and it is a pleasant ramble through this most attractive and little-known corner of Normandy. Having crossed the Bec, you then cross the River Risle, and after it, its other tributary, the Authou. The route wends its way uphill through woodland, across open countryside, through pretty villages, past a water-mill, an old church, a château and all the rest. That almost the entire route is on a Grande Randonnée is a testament to its merit. The final stretch in Brionne is along the riverside, with some classic scenes of half-timbered buildings beside the water.

The Walk

1. Leaving the cross-roads in the centre of town, take the Rue de Maréchal Foch, which takes you over the river, with the *donjon* ahead on its hill. Once over the river bridge, take a narrow road almost opposite, the Rue des Canadiens, waymarked as a Grande Randonnée. In about 100 metres, turn right on the Sente du Vieux-Château, which climbs past the *donjon* (go up to it from here if you want to see the view). Past the *donjon,* turn left and then again take the next turning on the left. This is the Côte de Calleville, and it descends to meet a road (the Rue des Canadiens again) at the bottom. Cross this road to a footpath about 10 metres to the right on the other side. A sign tells you this is the GR 224 *rive droite*. At the bottom of this track, turn left on the road to meet the main road. Turn right and walk under the overpass to a junction.

2. Here turn right in the direction of la Briquerie. The road climbs to meet the by-pass, but about 150 metres before reaching it, take a track doubling back on the left, climbing up behind the houses. Follow this well-waymarked track through the woods to arrive at another road on which you continue ahead to a T-junction. Here turn right and climb uphill into the forest. At a track junction take the centre of the three ways – just follow the excellent waymarking. The track continues between stands of coniferous and deciduous trees and eventually begins to descend. Soon you can see the 15th-century tower of St. Nicolas through the trees. At length you reach a road.

3. Turn right on the road to cross the valley with good views across the fields to the abbey on the right. Walk up through the village,

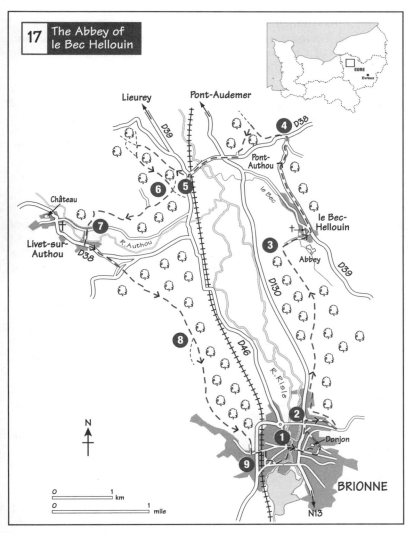

passing the entrance to the abbey and the crêperie opposite. Continue past the church to the main road, which you cross directly to a narrow road opposite. This climbs steadily and passes the cemetery (approx. 1km.) Shortly afterwards a road joins from the right and you go on to meet the main road, the D38.

4. Here, turn left and, in about 50 metres, take a track on the right along the edge of the woods. After about 10 minutes walking, just before a farm building on the right, leave the Grande Randonnée and take a grassy track on the left heading downhill. This section of the route is waymarked in yellow. This is a particularly pretty stretch of woodland. The path comes out beside the cemetery, after which you meet the D38 again. Turn right on the road and keep ahead at the cross-roads to cross the valley of the Risle in the village of Pont-Authou.

5. After crossing the railway, turn left briefly, and then double back to the right behind the restaurant. The path climbs steeply into the woods again, and there are good views into the valley on the right. At the top of the hill you reach a cross-roads of major tracks, with the *rive gauche* (left bank) branch of the GR224 coming in from the right. Turn left here, and in about 200 metres, again bear left, now following the white on red waymarks of the Grande Randonnée. A further 15 minutes walking brings you to another four-way junction as the path descends.

6. Turn right at this one. Suddenly there is a complete absence of waymarks but after 5 minutes or so they return to reassure you. At a cross-roads with a house on the right you continue ahead. The path now runs along the forest edge with open fields on the right and you come to yet another cross-tracks. This time turn left and then descend very steeply to a cross-roads at the bottom of the hill.

7. At this cross-roads you have a choice. Continuing ahead, you cross the river in the pretty village of Livet-sur-Authou and on the far side, meet the D38. Alternatively, adding a kilometre to your journey, you can turn right to reach the church at Livet-sur-Authou. Opposite it, there is a fine 19th century château and an old mill. Turn left at the church and you are on the D38, soon to rejoin those who crossed the river directly.

Whatever you did at Point 7, you will soon pass a bar/café on the D38 – this may be more than welcome! Continue along the road to cross a stream on a little brick bridge, and then, at the cross-roads, turn right on the Rue de Bretigny. This climbs and at the edge of the woods, comes to a junction with two cross roads. Go straight ahead and up the very steep track into the woods. At the top of the hill, beside a hut, the track turns right and immediately left. It is now a pleasant track with open fields on the right.

8. Coming to the lawns of a house on the right, fork left, passing a board announcing *La Vigneron*. At the next fork, go right, still following the waymarks. At the cross-roads continue straight ahead, and this is now a long easy track with some good views over the valley. As the path descends, take a sunken track on the right heading steeply downhill. At the road at the bottom, turn right to reach the main road.

9. Here turn left, and at the cross-roads, go straight ahead towards the railway. Cross over the railway, and turn immediately right to

reach the church. In front of the church turn left and walk down under the lime trees beside the lawns. At the main road at the bottom, cross straight over – the route is still waymarked in white on red. Walk down this short road and turn left at the bottom. You are now beside the river and heading towards the *donjon* on its hill. Cross the footbridge over an arm of the river and continue on the attractive riverside path to reach the main bridge in the town again. Turn left along the main street to the cross-roads from where you started.

More Walks in the Area

If you are spending some time in this region, go along to the interesting Office de Tourisme in Brionne (in a restored *pressoir,* or pressing house) where you can pick up the leaflet *Bienvenue autour de la Risle Brionnaise.* This gives you 13 circuits in the immediate vicinity of Brionne. The walk here is one of them. Other interesting ones include the 14.5km *Circuit des Lisières,* starting from the village of Harcourt (passing the Château de Beauficel, the Abbaye du Parc, and several typical half-timbered villages), and, from le Bec-Hellouin, the 10km *Circuit des Bénédictins* (passing the Monastère Ste. Françoise-Roumaine). And if you didn't manage the diversion at Point 7 on this walk, take the short 7km circuit from the pretty village of Livet-sur-Authou, passing five mills and two lavoirs along the river.

Continuing the monastic theme, there is an interesting 14km circuit at Bernay, 10km south-west of Brionne on the River Charentonne. You could visit the abbey-church before you set off. The route is described on the leaflet *Vallées de Risle et de la Charentonne,* a free leaflet that also details the Bec-Hellouin walk. The text is in French but the map and the waymarking on the ground are good.

For more walking in this area, think of getting the Topoguide *L'Eure à pied (Ref. D027).* This Topoguide is only available in French, but the maps are good and the routes in a Topoguide are generally well-waymarked. One interesting nearby circuit is that through the forest at Montfort-sur-Risle, downstream from Brionne, a mixed forest with some fine sequoias and an interesting *sentier botanique.* And, of course, the Topoguide contains another 40 or so excellent routes in the *département* of Eure – quite enough to be going on with.

Places of interest nearby

At the Abbey of le Bec Hellouin, guided tours take place at least three times a day throughout the year. Only a few crumbling stones of the old abbey church remain, but the new abbey church dates from the time of the Maurists in the 17th century. The cloisters are modelled on those at Monte Casino in Italy. The oldest building is the 15th century *Tour St. Nicolas,* where, on a plaque on the wall, are detailed the English clergy trained here in the 11th and 12th centuries. And if you are interested in visiting more abbeys, get hold of the free leaflet *La Route des Abbayes* from any Tourist Information.

The Musée de la Musique Mécanique is situated in the Rue Lanfranc, merely a stone's throw from the Abbey of le Bec Hellouin. If you are fascinated by phonographs, pianolas, dance organs, etc, it is well worth a visit. Guided tours only are possible – they take place morning and afternoon in high season, afternoons only in April, May and September.

6km south-east of Brionne is the Château d'Harcourt. In its grounds are arboretum, shrubbery, orchard and forest – all with exotic specimens. You could combine a visit here with a short walk – apart from the route mentioned in the More Walks section, a short circuit of 6km passes the entrance to the château. Get the leaflet *Bienvenue autour de la Risle Brionnaise*.

Eure

18. La Ferrière and the valley of the Risle

The attractive half-timbered town of la Ferrière is well off the usual tourist trail. From here you walk through the green valley of the River Risle, a fertile land of farms, apple orchards and delightful old villages.

Grade: Easy

Distance: 12km (7½ miles)

Time: 3½ hours

Map: The route crosses two IGN Série Bleue maps, 1913 0 and 1914 0

Start and finish: Place de la Halle (the town square) at La Ferrière

How to get there: La Ferrière lies on the D140 between Bernay and Conches-en-Ouche. At its heart is a large covered market hall, with plenty of parking all around.

Refreshment: There are several bar/restaurants in La Ferrière, but none on route.

Notes: This walk is mainly on good tracks and little-used country roads. Trainers should be adequate footwear – although in winter or after very wet weather boots might be appreciated. Carry drink with you – and note that there is not a great deal of shade on a sunny day, so take precautions.

Waymarking: The first half of the route is waymarked in yellow, after which you join the GR 224 with its white on red waymarking.

Introduction

Eure is surely the *département* of Normandy least known to tourists – of the region south of the River Seine, little appears in the guide books. It's a place you will need to discover for yourself. Eure is surprisingly the most wooded part of Normandy – forest occupies 20 % of its territory. South-west of the Seine, the land forms a limestone plateau where cereal crops grow on the open prairies: the plateau is cut by several almost-parallel rivers flowing north to join the Seine. The River Eure in the east is succeeded by the Iton and then the Risle, which itself is joined by the Charentonne. Each valley is an oasis, a green wooded belt of farms, fields, villages and water-mills, a glimpse of traditional countryside unchanged over the years.

This walk is a simple ramble in the valley of the Risle, a river that arises in the southern hills of Orne and meets the Seine only just before it reaches the sea near Honfleur. On its long journey it passes some interesting sights – the great Abbey of le Bec Hellouin (see Walk 17) and the 'Venice of Normandy', Pont-Audemer. La Ferrière is not quite in that league, but nevertheless, it is a pretty flower-decked little town of half-timbered buildings gathered around a large 14th century covered market hall. An arm of the river running through the back streets provides some delightful scenes worth seeking out. Narrow alleys between old half-timbered houses lead to tiny bridges garlanded with flowers. You wonder who keeps all this so beautifully! La Ferrière was a town of craftsmen when the iron industry in this region flourished way back in the 17ᵗʰ and 18ᵗʰ centuries. Looking around the houses you can still see a little of their wrought iron handiwork.

Leaving La Ferrière, the route wanders up hill and down dale, past fields, farms, woodland and villages before descending to cross the Risle beside an old water-mill. A little farther on, the hamlet of la Hungerie invites you to share its view – a long look down the valley of the winding river to where the spire and grey roofs of the tiny village of Champignolles thrust themselves above the trees. Peacefully grazing cattle and apple orchards complete the scene. From Champignolles the way home is an undemanding track beside the water-meadows – leaving you plenty of energy to explore La Ferrière before you leave.

The Walk

1. Leaving the square with the covered market, walk up to the church and turn right on the Rue Jean-Pothin. Cross over the river bridge and turn left, briefly following the direction of the Grande Randonnée. After passing the tennis courts (below the Église d'Ajou), take a metalled road climbing uphill on the right. From this point you are following yellow waymarks – but there aren't that many. The metalled road becomes rough surfaced, and at the fork at the top of the hill you take the grassy track to the left. This track now runs beside a field, through woodland and beside another field before reaching a tarmacked road.

2. Turn left on this road and keep to it as far as the cross-roads in the village of St.-Aubin-sur-Risle. Here, turn right and follow this wider road (with care, as it is not without traffic) uphill. The road corners sharp left, and passes a junction where the road to la Thevray goes off to the right. 10 minutes or so past this junction, just before the sign announcing the village of la Bonnelière, take a grassy track on the left, waymarked in yellow. This pleasant track runs under the trees and beside fields of grazing cattle. At the fork you keep right and continue on the obvious track winding in and out of woodland. The track crosses a small road and continues again between fields. Eventually you reach a small wood and through it descend to join another road.

3. Turn right on this road, which climbs uphill. At the T-junction, turn left and keep to the road through the village of Rubremont as far as the next T-junction (ignore all the yellow waymarking on side tracks – it belongs to other routes in this area).

4. At the T-junction, turn left in the direction of Valmont and Quincampoix. This road winds between the scattered houses of

The abbey at Jumièges (walk 25)

The colourful old dock (vieux bassin) at Honfleur (walk 11)

Val Pollet (walk 26)

Monet's house at Giverny (walk 20)

The village of le Bec-Hellouin, dominated by the tower of St. Nicolas (walk 17)

Dovecote at the Abbaye de Mortemer, Lyons-la-Forêt (walk 21)

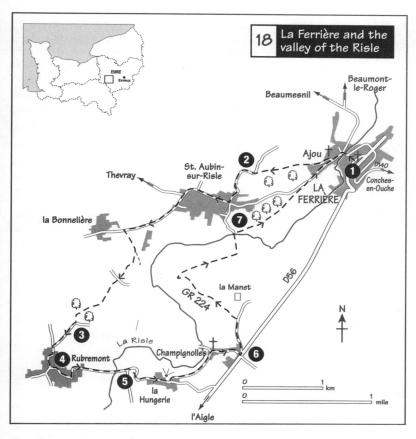

18 La Ferrière and the valley of the Risle

the village and makes a sharp left-hand turn followed by a sharp right. Ignore all the odd waymarking you see around. Keep to the road, which descends and crosses the River Risle. A big old watermill stands beside the river on your right.

5. Just after the bridge you come to a road junction where white on red flashes are apparent on the trees. The Grande Randonnée – proper waymarking at last! Now follow those waymarks up the bank to the left. This short path under the trees merely cuts off a corner of the road. Joining the road again, you turn left and continue into the village of la Hungerie. Just before the cross-roads there is a classic view on the left across the valley of the Risle to the church in the village of Champignolles. At the cross-roads, turn left on a rough road that dips into the valley. There are still fine views ahead of you. This very pleasant road takes you all the way to Champignolles beside the river. In this most attractive little village, do not cross the river, but continue ahead up the hill past the church to reach the main road.

6. Just as you arrive at the main road, turn sharply back to the left, on a rough road still marked as a Grande Randonnée. Ahead of you is the rather grand half-timbered manor of le Manet, and, to its left, a little chapel. The track now swings left and begins the descent into the valley again. At the bottom of the hill the track bears right and runs along the edge of a flat field extending to the river. In mid-field, the path turns left and runs behind a hedge to cross the river.

7. On the far side of the river turn right. Keep straight ahead on the track, leaving the road to double back behind you. The track follows the edge of the flat water-meadows and you can see the spire of the church at La Ferrière guiding you home. The track becomes a lane and then climbs to join the D 35. Keep straight on into the town and retrace your steps across the river bridge to return to the market hall.

More Walks in the Area

Two waymarked circuits in the valley of the Risle start from the covered hall at La Ferrière – a board on its wall tells you about them. The walk you have just taken is one of the routes. Going in the opposite direction, downstream, there is an 18km largely forested circuit whose turning point is the splendid farm-manor of Val-Gallerand. You can get details of this from any Office de Tourisme in the region (the nearest is at Conches-en-Ouche, which is worth a visit anyway). The route is contained in the Topoguide *L'Eure à Pied (Ref. D027)* and also in a volume entitled *Promenades et Randonnées dans l'Eure*. The latter offers you 61 circuits in Eure. Unfortunately the numbering seems rather muddled and it's difficult to work out what is included – not all the circuits on the main map, anyway. Nevertheless, the individual maps can be followed easily – and surprisingly, a few of the walks have been translated into English!

Much more visually appealing is a series of leaflets published by the Conseil General de l'Eure entitled *L'Eure au rythme des vallées*. A handful of routes are described in each valley – by and large they are the best of the routes appearing in the two publications named above. The next valley to the east, that of the Iton, is full of interesting walks. The Iton is a curious river that disappears underground at Villalet only to surge forth again 10km farther north at Gisolles. Four circuits are described south of Villalet in the leaflet *Val d'Iton, Rouloir et Vallée d'Avre*. But to find a walk in the dry part of the valley you will have to go to the Topoguide for the route *Le Sec-Iton*.

The area around La Ferrière is also given the title Pays d'Ouche. The capital of the Ouche is the town of Conches, 14km east of La Ferrière. The town itself is fascinating (see the Places of Interest section), but you might like to combine your visit with a walk described in both the topoguide and on the leaflet named above, the circuit of *La*

Half-timbered houses in La Ferrière

Vallée du Rouloir. This is a route of 14km that drops from the heights of Conches to wander through the wooded valley of the River Rouloir and passes the hamlet of Haute-Croisille where buildings date from the 12th century.

And finally, you can always follow the perfectly waymarked Grande Randonnée, the GR 224. This heads north along the valley of the Risle – you can follow it all the way to the sea. But for shorter stretches, equip yourself with the local IGN Série Bleue maps and follow the white on red flashes. If you don't want to retrace your footsteps to reach your car again, get a taxi to take you one way. Any Office de Tourisme will help. A suitable stretch would be La Ferrière to Beaumont-le-Roget, about 14km, but you might like to double the distance and go on to Bernay. The whole route of the GR 224 is described in the Topoguide *Vallées et forêts de l'Eure (Ref. 271)* – if you are staying in the area, it is well worth having.

Places of interest nearby

The biggest attraction of the Ouche is the Château de Beaumesnil, the 'Versailles of Normandy'. Built in 1640 in the reign of Louis XIII, this ornate brick and stone mansion is surrounded by moat and 80 hectares of woods and formal gardens landscaped by La Quintinie. He worked with Le Notre at Versailles – and the influence is obvious. Inside there is a fine collection of 17th- and 18th-century books and an exhibition of bookbinding. Beaumesnil is 7km north-west of La Ferrière. The château is open every day in July and August and on other selected days between Easter and September – enquire at the Office de Tourisme.

The town of Conches-en-Ouche stands on a high spur of land almost encircled by the River Rouloir 140 metres below. Such a spot would naturally have had its fortifications – the ivy-clad remains of the 11th-century castle keep now make an attractive scene in front of the Gothic doorway of the Town Hall. From the gardens there are fine views of the river below – and across to the medieval church of St. Foy above the precipice. The stained glass windows in this church date from the early 16th century and are said to be some of the finest in Normandy. Conches acquired its name from Conques in Aquitaine, a town on the pilgrim route from le Puy to Santiago de Compostela. One Roger de Tosny visited it in 1034 on his way back from the Spanish wars. While there he came across the relics of St Foy and brought them back to found a church in the town of Châtillon – which he then renamed. Conches is also noted for its wrought iron work. You may have noticed a huge wrought iron tableau of three pilgrims walking towards a shell (Coquille St. Jacques) on one of the approach roads to the town.

19. Les Andelys and the Château Gaillard

A relic of English rule in Normandy, the impressive hilltop Château Gaillard still commands the meandering Seine on its approach to Rouen From the old town of Petit Andely beside the river, this short walk takes you up the hill behind the château for one of the finest views in Normandy.

Grade: Easy – but there is a sustained climb at one point.

Distance: 8km (5 miles). The more energetic will find an extension in the More Walks section.

Time: 2 hours

Map: IGN TOP 25 2012 OT

Start and finish: The banks of the Seine at Petit Andely

How to get there: Les Andelys (Grand and Petit) are twin towns on the north bank of the Seine, south-east of Rouen. Leave the A13 Paris-Rouen Autoroute at Junction 17 and head north for 12km., crossing the Seine. There is parking in the square beside the church at Petit Andely. From here the Rue de la Tour will lead you down to the Seine.

Refreshments: There are eating houses of all kinds in Les Andelys.

Notes: This walk is entirely on minor roads and well-surfaced tracks – trainers would be suitable footwear. The only possible difficulty is the fairly steep climb out of the town. The treat comes near the end – the view is magnificent, so don't forget the camera. When you get down to the level of the château itself, a special viewing platform has been provided. This is only a brief walk, so you should have plenty of time to look round Château Gaillard at the end if you wish (for a small entrance fee). But if you prefer more exercise – look to the More Walks section.

Waymarking: The route is waymarked in blue at first, and later in the white on red colours of the Grande Randonnée. The town section is not waymarked.

Introduction

Way back in 1196, Richard the Lionheart was Duke of Normandy as well as King of England. When he got wind of the French king Philippe-Auguste's interest in Rouen, he knew he must bar his route of access – the River Seine. High on the cliffs at a bend in the river he built the supposedly impenetrable Château Gaillard. Legend has it that the vast fortress took only one year to build – 800 years on the majestic ruins still crown the hill. The fortification took the form of an outer stronghold surrounded by a moat. It was approached across a drawbridge from a triangular fortress guarded by five towers. This lesser fortress was connected to the slopes behind by just a narrow passage, the only vulnerable point. At first Philip-Auguste camped on the hills behind with the idea of starving out the English. But they had food supplies for years and it became apparent that another plan was needed. The French began to fill the moat with earth and trees and in doing so, undermined one of the towers of the access fort, which fell. Now they were ready for the main fortress – and they were able to invade through the weakest point, the latrines! Three months later Philippe-Auguste took Rouen and a year later Normandy was under French rule.

As you might expect, Château Gaillard has some tremendous views over the Seine. A little higher up the hill, the ruined château itself is in the picture – a photographer's dream! But the walk sets out far below in the grassy spaces beside the river at Petit Andely. It's a popular spot to take a picnic, looking out to the Île du Château and watching the huge barges making their way along the Seine. Beside the river is the old Hôpital St Jacques and from here you follow a stream that winds its way through the back streets of the town. Climbing above it, you reach the very old *beffroi* (bell tower) before descending to the Église Notre-Dame, dating from the 13th century, and crossing the second stream of the valley. A fairly strenuous climb leads you to a pretty path through the woods high above the Seine. When you emerge on to the meadows, there is suddenly this marvellous view of the white crumbling ruins of Château Gaillard. Way below is the town of Petit Andely with its fine church spire, and past it flows the Seine, curving away into the distance beneath cliffs of white chalk. For a small fee you can cross the footbridge into the château to appreciate its superb command of the river. Otherwise, do not leave without visiting the viewing platform below the château for a last lingering look over the Seine at Petit Andely.

The Walk

1. Facing the Seine across the grassy lawns, turn right and take the pedestrian path in front of the superb river-front residences. At its end, you see ahead the 18th century buildings of the Hôpital Saint-Jacques. Here double back to the right and take the road between the half-timbered houses to reach the main road. Cross straight over this and take the Promenade des Prés opposite. Now you meet the first blue waymarks as you continue ahead to join the stream on your left. This is the Ruisseau du Grand-Rang and you follow its pleasant course for around a kilometre, as it slips quietly through the back streets of the town. Several small roads are crossed but the blue waymarks lead you on.

2. When you can follow the stream no longer because you arrive at a cross road, turn left. At its end, turn right on to the Rue de la Madeleine. A mere 10 metres or so along this road, find an alley on the

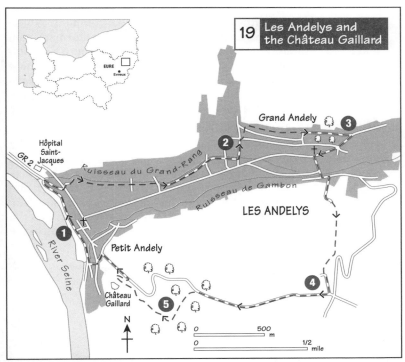

19 Les Andelys and the Château Gaillard

Grand Andely

LES ANDELYS

Petit Andely

Château Gaillard

Hôpital Saint-Jacques

GR 2

Ruisseau du Grand-Rang

Ruisseau de Gambon

River Seine

N

0   500
              m
0   1/2
                   mile

left, the Chemin de l'Horloge. The alley leads you uphill between old houses to come out beneath the clock tower. Cross directly over the old narrow street to continue up the alleyway and come out on the Rue des Remparts. Turn right and walk past the remains of the old town ramparts. At the end of the road, continue into the tree-lined Boulevard du Chapitre, which meets the main road. (Ignore the blue waymarks inviting you to turn up the rough road on the left – this is the official described route, but the climb and descent along main roads has little to recommend it)

3. At the main road, turn right and continue as far as the impressive Église Notre-Dame. Here, cross over the road, and take the road almost opposite, the Rue Pasteur. This leads you across the bridge over the Grand-Rang and then swings left. Now take the first road on the right sign-posted to the Cimetière Val St. Jean. The road now climbs past the cemetery, after which a broad track leads you on uphill. After a fairly steep climb under the trees, you come out beside a farm and then reach a tarmacked road.

4. Here turn right (away from the cross-roads) and continue along the hilltop past the Sports ground. A Grande Randonnée (GR 2) joins you from the left. As the road reaches the woodland, take a track on the left marked with the white on red flashes of the GR. A

Parcours de Santé (Fitness Course) keeps you company as you walk on under the beech trees. After the horizontal bars, you leave the Parcours and continue ahead and then sharp right following the waymarks. Coming out to a grassy field, there is a fine view of the Seine and Petit Andely. Turn left here and walk downhill on the grassy slope – Château Gaillard peeps through the trees. Soon the whole château is in view ahead of you with a fine panorama behind – a place to stop awhile.

5. Now continue downhill, passing the château on your left. At the end, the track doubles back to the right and descends to the road below – but before you go down, you might like to visit the viewing platform ahead. When you get down to the road, turn left and bear left at the fork at the bottom of the hill. At the main road, turn left, and after about 20 metres, find a narrow road on the right, the Ruelle de la Grâce de Dieu. This short road soon returns you to the lawns beside the Seine.

Château Gaillard

More Walks in the Area

Another popular walk starting from Petit Andelys is the Circuit du Mont-Pivin. This route is well described in a leaflet entitled *Vallée de la Seine* – one of the excellent series *L'Eure au Rythme des Vallées*. The 9km route first follows the banks of the Seine and then returns across the heights of Mont-Pivin, from which there are again fine views of Château Gaillard. It is possible to combine this route with the walk of the text, making a day's walk of 17km But a shorter walk – or a shorter addition – would be to follow the green waymarks of the Mont-Pivin circuit along the banks of the Seine and inland to the village of Le Val

St.-Martin. From here you can follow the white on red waymarks of the GR 2 across the lower wooded slopes of Mont-Pivin to return to Petit Andely – a total distance of about 5km This route can clearly be seen on the leaflet named above (obtainable from the Office de Tourisme at Petit Andely), and on the IGN map of the region, 2012 OT.

The GR 2 winds its way along the hills on the right bank of the Seine and makes a very pleasant excursion in either direction from Les Andelys. A day's walk downstream from Les Andelys would probably take you as far as Herqueville, 18.5km (from where you could cross the river to Saint-Pierre-de-Vauvray, with more facilities). Since there are no easy connections here, you would need two cars – or you could enquire at the Office du Tourisme about taxis. The railway runs along the left bank of the Seine, so if you choose two places with both station and bridge, you can cross to the opposite bank for the GR 2. Upstream from Les Andelys, Vernon and Gaillon, 25km apart, would be such a choice. To explore the possibilities of the GR 2 along the length of the Seine (Triel to Le Havre), purchase the Topoguide *La Seine en Normandie (Ref. 201)*, available only in French. But if you want just a short section, it is easy to follow this Grande Randonnée using the appropriate IGN map and the excellent waymarking on the ground.

And finally, Giverny is just 22km up the Seine – see Walk 20, a short ramble in the hills behind Monet's house. If you have acquired the leaflet *Vallée de la Seine* mentioned above, you will also have the route of a longer (14km.) walk starting from the same place – take your choice.

Places of interest nearby

Following the banks of the Seine downstream for about 30km (but only about 20km by road), you arrive at the Écluses d'Amfreville – the huge locks below which the Seine is tidal. It is possible to walk across the footbridge here for a view of the Poses Dam on the far side of the river – and appreciate the special arrangements for migrating fish who would otherwise find their way barred by the mighty works of man. Above the Seine at Amfreville is a steep hill known as the Côte des Deux-Amants, from a story first told way back in the 12th century. Caliste, the daughter of the local Baron, was wandering in the forest when she was attacked by a wild beast – and she was saved by Raoul, the son of a Count. The two fell in love, but Baron Rulphe put a condition on their marriage – that Raoul should carry Caliste in his arms to the top of this hill. This he did – but at the top he collapsed and died of exhaustion. Caliste, overcome by grief, died beside him. The remorseful Baron buried them on the hill and built a chapel on the spot.

The Côte des Deux-Amants is a superb vantage point with views over the locks, barrage and winding river. And you don't have to follow Raoul's example in climbing the steep slope (although a GR goes that way) – a road will deliver you to the top.

Upstream from Les Andelys at Gaillon, a magnificent Renaissance château overlooks the Seine. Georges d'Amboise, a Cardinal under Louis XII, made a trip to Italy around 1500 – and was inspired by the architecture. Returning home to Gaillon, he built this château, the first example of Renaissance style in Normandy. The château is presently undergoing a lengthy restoration, but is open to the public in July and August.

An assortment of cruise boats ply the Seine – you can take anything from a simple afternoon on the river to a dinner dance or a whole week's cruise. Any Office de Tourisme can give you details. A popular starting point is Vernon, just up river from Les Andelys.

20. In Monet's footsteps at Giverny

Escape the crowds at Monet's home in Giverny and take to the hills where once the great man himself must have walked. High above the Seine the limestone grassland is rich in wild flowers and there are distant views of the river beneath its white cliffs.

Grade: Moderate

Distance: 5.5km (3½ miles). An extension is possible, making a total distance of 10km (6 ¼ miles)

Time: 1½ hours (double this if you take the extension)

Map: IGN Série Bleue 2113 O

Start and finish: Monet's house at Giverny

How to get there: From Vernon, cross the Seine and turn right, following signs to Giverny. Once in the village, you will have no problem finding the large car park opposite Monet's house.

Refreshment: There are several bars and restaurants in Giverny

Notes: In summer this brief walk can readily be undertaken in trainers, although stouter footwear may be preferable at other times. The walk is largely on grassy tracks along the slopes. This is not difficult terrain but some climbing and descending is involved. Even though this is a short walk, it's worth taking a drink on a hot day – and the slopes are largely exposed, so you may need sun-screen. For those with more time – and energy – an extension to this walk is described in the More Walks section.

Waymarking: Much of the route is on the Grande Randonnée of the Seine Valley, the GR 2, and so is waymarked in white on red. Elsewhere the route is waymarked in yellow.

Introduction

Monet's beautiful house and gardens in Giverny form one of the most visited tourist attractions in France, their popularity akin to that of the Eiffel Tower. If you choose to visit on a summer weekend, you will have no difficulty believing it! Nevertheless, this is a place not to be missed and if you come to Giverny, a walk will have to take second place to the tour.

Claude Monet arrived at Giverny in 1883. After many years of struggle, things were beginning to go well for him and he was able to afford this fine house near the Seine. He created here the home and garden of his dreams. It is the colours of the house that stick in the mind after a visit – the pink and bright green of the exterior, the vivid yellow and blue of the dining room and kitchen. The house is smaller than you might have guessed from the pictures – merely one room thick. Monet lived here with his own two children, his second wife and her six children – ten people! How did they all fit in? There are no original paintings in the house, just a huge collection of photographic

Monet's house at Giverny

reproductions gracing the walls of his studio. Perhaps more interesting are the Japanese drawings and ceramics that inspired his later work – and, of course, his garden. However many times you may have gazed at prints of the Water Lilies and however numerous the throng sharing the scene with you, you will still be bowled over by the beauty of that lily pond with its graceful bridge.

When you have finished the tour you will be more than ready for an escape to the wilds. This walk leads you out on to the chalk slopes over-looking the Seine – where you are treading in the steps of the master. Monet was said to wander these paths in his search for the subjects of his paintings. Wild flowers are abundant on the grassy banks and on a sunny day the butterflies are out in force. The route dips in and out of woodland and from the wide grassy tracks you can see the distant laden barges making their way along the Seine. Below you the grey-spired church at Giverny looks out over the valley. Monet is buried in this churchyard in a simple family grave – there are no signs directing you to it, and few people manage to walk the half kilometre or so from the house. On your return down the village street you will pass the other attraction in Giverny, the Musée d'Art Américain. This owes its existence to a group of American artists who arrived here in the late 19th century, attracted by Monet's band of impressionists – it is said that Monet ignored them. But the exhibition here is interesting and includes many scenes of the Giverny of their day – a fitting end to the walk.

The Walk

1. Leaving the car park facing Monet's House, turn left and walk along the road away from the village. Now turn left on the Rue du Château d'Eau, which climbs to reach the Rue Hélène Pillon. At this junction turn right, now following yellow, green and white on red (GR) waymarks. The road becomes a pleasant broad grassy track with distant views – but don't relax too much!

2. Just as the track begins to descend, the Grande Randonnée turns sharply and makes a scramble up the bank on your left. Half way up the slope there is a track junction at which you turn right, still following the white on red flashes of the GR. This is now a beautiful track across the limestone slopes. The shrubs and groups of trees give way to woodland and you descend to a track junction at the bottom of a hill

3. Here you leave the Grande Randonnée (going right) and turn left, now following yellow waymarks. At the track junction at the top of the hill, bear left and, reaching the open field, turn right along the woodland edge. After about 300 metres, you reach a track junction

4. The possible extension to the route begins here – see the More Walks section.

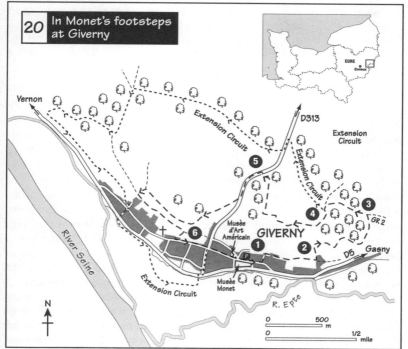

To continue with the main walk, turn left here along the edge of another field. Mid-way along, a post with a yellow waymark invites you to turn right and cross the field. On reaching the field edge in front of more woodland, turn right again, now skirting the third side of the field. The track here is less definite. Half way along this side, look for a broad track through the woods going steeply downhill. It is waymarked in yellow. The track comes down to a tarmacked road.

5. Turn left on this road and walk downhill for about 300 metres to where the road begins a right-hand bend. Now take a broad track on the right, running between fences. At the track junction in about 250 metres, you keep straight ahead – and are again joined by the Grande Randonnée. Look for the ostrich farm below you on the left. You are now on a lovely flower-banked track with wide views across the Seine. Barges glide slowly down the river, while double-decker trains race along the banks under the cliffs on the far side. Below you, the little church at Giverny surveys the scene.

6. After passing above the church, take a track (now waymarked in yellow) heading down the bank on the left. In 150 metres or so, before the house, turn left again and follow yet another grassy track towards Giverny. Again pass above the church and, just beyond the wire enclosure, take a narrow track heading downhill on the right (not waymarked). This brings you to the main road through the village. The church is just a few metres along on the right if you choose to seek the grave of the Monet family. Otherwise, turn left and keep straight ahead to pass the Musée d'Art Américain and return to the car park.

More Walks in the Area

This is only a short walk, all you may have time for after a visit to the house and gardens. But if you fancy something a bit more substantial, an extension is possible, making a total length of 10km The whole route can be found on the leaflet *L'Eure au rythme des Vallées – Vallée de la Seine*, a leaflet you should be able to find in any Tourist Office in the *département* of Eure. The extension starts at point 4 on this route, when instead of crossing the field, you continue on the track along the edge of the wood to reach the road. Following yellow waymarks, you turn left here, and then twice right, skirting another woodland edge to rejoin the GR 2. There is a fine viewpoint at the Belvédère de la Grosse-Pierre before descending to return along the track of an old railway. The extension is marked on the sketch map of this walk.

If you are staying in the area for a while, it might be worth acquiring the Topoguide *L'Eure à pied (Ref. D027)*, which describes 41 different walks in the *département* of Eure. Even if you don't speak a word of French you can follow the routes in this book – they are all well waymarked and the maps are excellent. A 16km circuit starts from Pressagny-l'Orgueilleux, just downstream from Giverny. This is a splendidly varied walk, heading off into the forest, following the River Catenay through its deep valley and returning along the banks of the Seine itself.

Across the river from Giverny at Vernon, the Office de Tourisme has produced its own set of 4 walking leaflets. These have the merit of being free, but you would probably need some command of French to follow the routes as there is no waymarking on the ground. The text is accompanied by sketch maps only. Nevertheless, the 12km route entitled *Vernon – Hameau de Normandie* should not prove too difficult. It heads into the woods south of Vernon, picks up the GR 26 (well waymarked) and returns along the towpath of the Seine.

Places of interest nearby

The Musée Claude Monet – Monet's house, gardens and former studio – is open to the public every day except Monday from 1st April to 31st October. If you have any choice in the matter, avoid summer weekends. The Musée is now owned by the *Fondation Claude Monet* who, for a very modest sum, simply allow you free access to the house and gardens. If you are here at a quiet time you can easily take a couple of hours over it all. Even the most dedicated walker will want to make this visit before setting out on the trail.

Just along the road from the Musée Claude Monet is the Musée d'Art Américain. The museums share the same opening dates and times (10 a.m. to 6 p.m.). This museum displays the work of American artists in France around the end of the 19th century (Mary Cassatt and Lila Cabot Perry among many others) – and there is an annual series of temporary exhibitions.

Wandering around the village of Giverny, you will find several studios of modern day artists – along with those of sculptors and other craftsmen. A couple of premises invite you to taste – and buy – the traditional produce of Normandy. Interspersed in all this is the odd restaurant and café. It's a scene to browse in – although you may wonder what the indigenous population thinks of it all.

Leaving Giverny behind and travelling up river, yet another château dominates the Seine – the Château de la Roche-Guyon (don't get confused here – there are two chateaux downstream with similar names – the château at Gaillon and the Château Gaillard at Les Andelys). The Château de la Roche-Guyon was built in the 12th century as a sort of border-post between Normandy and Île-de-France. Having defended its way through the centuries, it was the Duke of Rochefoucauld who in the 1700s was responsible for its metamorphosis. He gave it fine stables, pavilions and terraces, a dovecote and an orangerie under the rock. Now a blend of medieval fortress and grand château, it is open to visitors throughout the year.

21. Colourful Lyons-la-Forêt

The half-timbered buildings and covered medieval hall at Lyons make it one of the most picturesque towns in Normandy. Surrounding the town, the hills are clad in forest of oak and beech, once the hunting-ground of the Dukes of Normandy. Enjoy this walk in the woods, and the fine town at its heart.

Grade: Moderate

Distance: 11.5km (8¼ miles). It is possible to divide the walk into two circuits of 7 and 6km respectively.

Time: 4 hours for whole route

Map: IGN TOP 25 2111 OT. This walk (with only one or two variations) is described in a leaflet *Pays de Lyons-Andelle* – one of the series *L'Eure au rythme des vallées*. If you can get hold of this, the map given is quite adequate.

Start and finish: The market hall at Lyons-la-Forêt

How to get there: About 30km east of Rouen, the Forest of Lyons lies between the N31 and the N14. The town of Lyons-la-Forêt is at its heart. There is parking near the Post Office, just along from the central square (Place Benserade), on the road to Beauficel.

Refreshment: Lyons-la-Forêt is well-supplied with restaurants and cafés.

Notes: This is a fine walk through the forest – cool on a hot summer's day, but muddy underfoot in winter. Take a drink with you as there is no refreshment en route. The Forêt de Lyons unfortunately suffered much damage in the terrible storm in the last days of 1999. The French authorities are working hard to open all paths again as soon as possible but this may take time. The route here has been chosen to avoid the worst trouble and was clear in all except one short stretch in the summer of 2000.

Waymarking: The route is waymarked in red throughout.

Introduction

In the best traditions of Normandy, the multi-coloured half-timbered buildings of Lyons-la-Forêt are jumbled around an old market hall festooned with bright geraniums. Typically Flaubertian, the French rush along to Lyons every time they want to film a new version of *Madame Bovary*. The fountain in the square is a legacy of the last shooting in 1990. A plaque on a tall half-timbered residence just off the square proclaims that Ravel lived here for a while, and during his residence composed *Le Tombeau de Couperin* and orchestrated Mussorgsky's *Pictures from an Exhibition*. Lyons-la-Forêt is evidently well-preserved – and very photogenic.

Lyons stands above the River Lieure (the Rieule of *Madame Bovary*), and all around is the vast forest of oak and beech. Within its

Ravel's house at Lyons-la-Forêt

confines are a couple of châteaux, an abbey, several ancient wayside chapels, springs with reputedly healing powers and some remarkably aged trees – all connected by a network of forest tracks. The walk here simply encircles the town of Lyons and can easily be divided into two shorter circuits. The route is by no means entirely in forest, but rather weaves its way in and out of woodland and pastureland, meanders up and down hills and follows a long track through the valley of the Lieure. At one point you can choose to make a detour to the Chêne St. Jean (St. John's Oak), a huge tree with a trunk circumference of 5 metres. For the energetic, the path continues up the hill to the tiny old Chapelle St. Jean. Returning again through the valley to Lyons, you pass the Eglise St. Denis famous for its statues in wood (what else around here?) and pass below the old walls to cross the river at the 'Square des Trois Moulins'. The three mills in question have been restored and are now most attractive residences. From here you can opt for a quick return to town – or to continue with the woodland wander, with some fine views for reward.

The Walk

1. From the market hall, take the road towards Beauficel. In about 100 m. you come to the Post Office on the right hand side (there is a car park behind it). From here, bear right and climb on the Chemin de la Croix-Mesnil. A board at the foot of the hill points you to the *Circuit de la Fontaineresse* and you will see (occasional!) red waymarks. Continue on this broad gravel track to pass the manor of Croix-Mesnil on your left. At the road, turn right and in about 200 m. reach the main road, the D2.

2. Cross straight over the D2 to a track opposite. In about 50 metres,

bear right on a grassy track going downhill. The track takes a sharp corner to the left and continues descending through the woodland. In about 800 metres, you reach another main road, this time the D 321 (The original waymarked route left the grassy track about 200 metres before the road, and turned left, climbing alongside the deep valley of a stream. At the time of writing this part of the forest was impassable due to storm damage. However, the route may be re-instated – it is marked on the sketch map).

3. Cross the road, turn left and walk along the grassy bank for about 300 metres to a lay-by. Here take the rough road on the right that takes you across the River Lieure. At the far side the track bends to the right – and here you will see the sign pointing you uphill to the Chapelle St. Jean – about 20 minutes away. Sadly the hill above here bore the brunt of *la Tempête*, and was inaccessible in the summer of 2000. Did the old oak itself survive? The path will almost certainly be opened again – its route has been shown on the sketch map.

4. Now continue on the broad track along the valley of the Lieure. Eventually it becomes tarmacked and you arrive at a road junction with the Église St. Denis up on your left. Turn right here and immediately cross the river on a bridge decked with flowers. A delightful street of half-timbered houses follows.

5. Here you can decide whether or not to add a further 6km to your route. Just before the road junction, a narrow road leads downhill on the left, signposted to the 'Square des Trois Moulins'. For those who wish to retire here, continue past this turning (although the Square des Trois Moulins is very picturesque – you might just like to have a look). At the road junction, turn right up the Rue de l'Hôtel de Ville to pass the Office du Tourisme and return to the central square and market hall.

To continue with the walk, take the road down to the Trois Moulins and again cross the river. Keep ahead on the track. This corners to the right (do not go ahead uphill) and emerges on the main road opposite the camping site.

6. Now walk uphill on the road to a left hand bend in about 350 metres. Here leave the main road and keep straight ahead (S.P. to Lorleau). After about 200 metres, turn right on a track, the Chemin de l'Étang. Continue to the edge of a field where the track forks.

7. Bear left for about 20 metres, and then bear right along the edge of the wood. Continue climbing under the trees with the field on your right. At the end of the second field the track turns right, again skirting the field along the woodland edge. At the top of the field the path again bears right. There seem to be quite a few red waymarks around, and even arrows on trees (these actually point

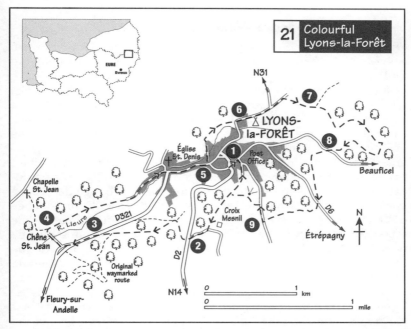

backwards as you are taking this circuit in the reverse of the described direction). At a fork in the track, bear left and then left again to cut off the woodland corner. Climb towards some large beeches beside a road.

8. At the road, turn right and after about 20 metres take a track on the left. A sign here tells you that you are on the *Promenade du Four à Chaux* (Lime-Kilns Walk – the lime-kilns are ahead of you in the wood). Follow this gravel track to reach a clearing at the edge of the wood. Here turn left and now keep straight ahead on the track along the forest edge. Eventually you reach another road. Cross straight over into an area of rough grassland opposite. Now continue straight ahead to the woodland corner, where a flight of steps leads you down into a gully in the wood. Climbing out of the gully, the obvious path leads you on through the wood to another shingly clearing. Here turn left to come down to a road.

9. Turn right on the road and walk downhill for about 200 metres, with forest on your right. Reaching the forest edge again on the left, immediately turn left to climb on a path through the trees. The path should be quite clear (although there was much storm damage here) and there are soon fine views across Lyons to the other side of the valley. Eventually the path comes down to a gravel road. Turn right here to return to the Post Office at Lyons-la-Forêt.

More Walks in the Area

On the edge of the forest, 4km south of Lyons, stand the ruins of the Abbaye de Mortemer. There's a lot more here than crumbling old buildings (see Places of Interest below) and the abbey site would make an interesting visit for all the family. While there you might like to take a family-sized walk – a circuit of 4km passes the door. Apart from a wander through the woodland, where there are some truly giant oak trees, there is a pleasant section above the stream with a visit to the Source Ste. Cathérine. For a small donation, Ste. Cathérine will guarantee to find you a husband within a year! For longer-legged families, the route can be extended to 8km to reach the pretty valley of St. Laurent. The first of these walks is described in the Topoguide *L'Eure à pied* and also in a booklet entitled *À pied dans l'Eure – Vallee d'Andelle, Forêt de Lyons, Pays de Gisors et Vexin Normand*. The second route is only in the booklet. Both these publications should be on sale at the Office de Tourisme at Lyons-la-Forêt (in the Rue de l'Hôtel de Ville) and elsewhere. Both routes are well waymarked on the ground so you should have no difficulty following them.

Along the western boundary of the forest flows the River Andelle. Several fine walks are described in this pretty valley where there is much of interest (see the Nearby Places section below). One of the most favoured walks is the 10km *Circuit du Bois de Bonnemare*, starting from the Château at Radepont, south-west of Lyons. The route also passes the Château of Bonnemare, the Abbey of Fontaine-Guérard and the very curious fire-ravaged *Filature de Monsieur Levavasseur* – the ruins of a factory once built like a cathedral (see below). For those wanting a longer walk, two other woodland circuits (19 and 25km.) also start from Radepont. All are described in the booklet *À pied dans l'Eure* (see above), but the popular *Bois de Bonnemare* walk also appears in the leaflet *L'Eure au rythme des vallées – Pays de Lyons-Andelle*.

Places of interest nearby

The Cistercian Abbaye de Mortemer is set in parkland with three lakes, where you can wander freely in the company of the ponies and deer – or if you prefer, take a ride on the little tourist train. Of the 12th century buildings, only a few ruins remain to be seen. But the 17th century convent building has been restored and now houses a museum of monastic life. In the atmospheric vaults, stories and legends of the abbey's past are told, using wax models with ghostly lighting and sound effects. The most famous spectre is apparently to be seen on the night of a full moon – the ghost of Mathilde, daughter of Henry I, a young lady whose amorous exploits offended her father's medieval propriety. He imprisoned her in this abbey – but died himself next year after eating infected lampreys from the lake. The abbey grounds welcome visitors every afternoon throughout the year, although the abbey itself is only open from Easter to September. August brings additional evenings of Son et Lumière. Overlooking the abbey grounds is a pleasant crêperie serving regional produce – but lampreys are off the menu.

Elsewhere in the forest there is plenty to see. At Fleury-la-Forêt, east of Lyons, there is a fine 17th-century château, and a little further on at Bosquentin is the *Musée de la Ferme et des Vieux Métiers* – a museum of rural crafts. This forest is renowned for its particularly large and aged trees, so don't leave without a quick visit to the Hêtre de Bunaudière (in the north-east, off the N31), a beech some 40 metres in height, and the Gros Chêne (south of Lyons), an oak 30 metres high with a trunk circumference of 4.8 metres.

Going west to the valley of the Andelle, the beautiful ruins of the Abbaye de Fontaine-Guérande stand in a lonely site beside the river. Further down the road are different ruins – the mock-Gothic octagonal-towered Filature de Monsieur Levavasseur was a spinning mill in the 19th century before being destroyed by fire. Up river, the old brick Château de Vascoeuil is worth a visit

The French may choose Lyons-la-Forêt for their film sets of *Madame Bovary*, but the recent BBC version was filmed in the little town of Ry, 15km north-west of Lyons. Flaubert had family connections with Ry and the sorry tale is said to be based on real events in that town – given the pseudonym Yonville l'Abbaye. Ry is entirely going along with this, providing a board in the car park to identify various scenes in the story. You can take a walk along the main street passing the doctor's house, the chemists shop, the town hall and just about anywhere else you can recall (it's best to read the book before you go). Beside the pretty river, the half-timbered buildings of an old cider-press house the *Musée d'Automates* (Museum of Animated Puppets). No fewer than 500 of these are in action here – and naturally, most are performing scenes from *Madame Bovary*.

Coastal path near Étretat (Walk 22)

Seine-Maritime

22. Seascapes at Étretat

The smooth-pebbled beach and arched chalk cliffs at Étretat create a scene that has inspired writers and artists over the centuries. This is a walk not-to-be-missed along one of the best-known coasts in Europe.

Grade: Moderate

Distance: 7km (4½ miles)

Time: 2 hours

Map: IGN Série Bleue 1710 E

Start and finish: The sea-front at Étretat

How to get there: Étretat is on the coast 20km north of Le Havre. There is a fair-sized car park (for which there is a charge) at the west end of the sea-front. But Étretat is a popular place in summer, and extra car parks are to be found on the outskirts of the town.

Refreshment: Étretat has a wealth of eating houses of all kinds.

Notes: This walk is mostly on grassy cliff-top paths, but includes a short woodland section, again on well-surfaced track. There are one or two climbs, but none are too strenuous. On a hot day, take a drink with you and put on the sun-screen – and the beach at Étretat, although pebbly, is popular for bathing, so add your costume. And finally – this coast is very photogenic, so don't forget the camera.

Waymarking: The cliff-top path is a Grande Randonnée, and so is marked with flashes of white on red. Elsewhere, the waymarking is yellow.

Introduction

The white shingle beach at Étretat is sheltered to east and west by high chalk cliffs, and in each direction the escarpment is pierced by an arch. To the east is the low Porte d'Amont (Upstream Gate), while to the west is perhaps the most famous seascape in Normandy, the Porte d'Aval (Downstream Gate) and l'Aiguille (The Needle). The play of light on these well-known formations – and on the other phenomena of this coast – attracted painters of the impressionist school in the latter half of the 19th century. Corot and Courbet were followed by Boudin and Monet in coming to capture these scenes on canvas. Writers were also drawn to the town. Guy de Maupassant spent his childhood here and later on wrote evocatively of Étretat in his novel *Une Vie*. Alexandre Dumas had a villa here, André Gide was married in Étretat and Victor Hugo also became a visitor. Maurice Leblanc, the creator of the tales of the 'gentleman-burglar' Arsène Lupin, made his home in the town and in his books gave vivid descriptions of this coast. His villa, Le Clos Lupin, is now open to visitors who come to experience a mysterious '45 minutes in the company of Arsène Lupin'. Another famous name to be linked with Étretat was that of the com-

Porte d'Aval and l'Aiguille

poser Offenbach – he built his own villa here in 1858. And Marie-Antoinette was yet one more – although she merely had her own oyster park at the foot of the cliffs.

But Étretat was not only for the artists. In the Belle Époque, the rich and famous of Paris also discovered Étretat, and made it their summer watering hole. Many of the fine villas of the town were seasonal residences, and some have belonged to the same family over seven or eight generations. At the height of its popularity as a *station balneaire*, Étretat's beach was actually divided into two – to the east were the summer visitors with their casino and bathing huts, to the west were the old fishing population with their boats and nets. It was forbidden to cross between! After the Second World War, sailing became a fashionable holiday pastime – and the visitors bought the boats of the fishermen, and even employed the locals to take them out to sea. So the class barriers broke down, but even today Étretat is second home to many families of Parisiens.

From Étretat, there are fine cliff walks in both directions. The walk here heads south and so climbs immediately to the cliff above the Porte d'Aval. Here there is a magnificent view across the bay to the Porte d'Amont, called by Maupassant the Petite Porte, and likened by him to an enormous elephant dipping his trunk in the water. On the cliff above stands the chapel of Notre-Dame-de-la-Garde, and behind the chapel, a spire like the gnomon of a giant sundial points to the western sky. In 1927, the French aviators Nungesser and Coli, heroes of the First World War, were the first to attempt the crossing of the Atlantic by plane. They never arrived – but this was the point at which they were last seen, crossing the French coast. Nearby there is a small museum telling the tale.

Looking west from the Aval cliff is another huge arch in the rock – the Manne Porte (Great Gate) – you might think this looks like an elephant's head complete with its eye. Walking between the Aval Cliff and the Manne Porte provides a close-up view of l'Aiguille, a stack 80 m. high rising from the swirling seas. At close quarters you can see the striations caused by layers of flint between the limestone.

When you leave the coast on this walk, the way home lies through the attractive Valleuse d'Antifer. This is a protected site, a deep wooded valley running out to the sea, noted for its population of wild flowers. The path from here climbs up through the woods to the golf course and you have yet more views of this splendid coast on the way home.

The Walk

1. From the western end of the sea-front an obvious path climbs to the cliffs above the Porte d'Aval. At the top there are various viewpoints from which to look out over the bay to the Porte d'Amont and ahead to the Manne Porte arch. Continuing, the path along the cliff-top is quite clear and soon you arrive above the Manne Porte. Keeping on down the coast, the next promontory is the Pointe de Courcine, and from here there are good views back to the arch of the Manne Porte, which looks quite different from this side. Ahead of you the harbour wall of the petrol port (Le Havre-Antifer) stretches out into the sea.

2. At the end of the golf course, the Grande Randonée turns off to the left, but you follow signs to the Valleuse d'Antifer, going straight on around the side of the valley. Heading downhill, you come to a road, which you cross directly. On the far side of the road, take a track that climbs out of the valley, bearing right and heading for the coast again. This path soon becomes a broad track climbing uphill. A path heads up to the cliff summit on your right, but unless you want another view of the coast, you can safely ignore it. At the top of the slope you come to a junction. The path to the right (towards the sea again) has yellow waymarks, but just disregard them and carry straight on maintaining the same direction.

3. Soon you arrive at a barrier before a hard-surfaced road. Again continue ahead on the road, and after about 200 metres, reach a junction in the village of la Place. Here turn left, and keep ahead on the road, passing some interesting properties. At the bottom of the hill, go through the barrier on the left to take the broad grassy track beside the trees. The barrier is waymarked, telling you that this is circuit no. 2. The track becomes stony as you descend beside some fine chestnut trees into the Valleuse d'Antifer.

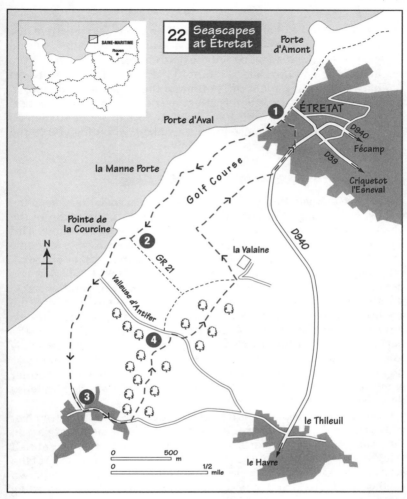

4. On reaching the road in the valley, turn right and continue uphill for about 250 metres to a small tarmacked parking area. Now turn left on the Chemin de Valaine (marked with a no. 2), which heads into the woodland. The path climbs through the trees and emerges between fields at the top.

5. Reaching a 5-way junction (4 tracks and a tarmacked road), you can see opposite the farm La Valaine, famous for its goats' cheese. Here take the track at right-angles to you on the left (not the double-back left). This track is heading towards the coast again. Coming to a T-junction beside a house (before the golf course), turn right. The grassy track continues behind the golf course and begins to descend with good views ahead. Soon the track becomes sunken between banks and surprisingly, you arrive at a metal barrier. At this point you can walk around either side to descend to the road below. At the bottom of the hill you reach the main road and turn left to return to the town. If you wish to get back to the car park at the bottom of the cliffs, take the narrow road on the left immediately after the entrance to 'Dormy House' – it is again marked with a no. 2. At the fork in about 40 metres, bear left, and a few more minutes walking will bring you to the sea-front car park.

More Walks in the Area

If you have enjoyed this walk you will be keen to walk the cliffs in the opposite direction. The coastal path east is the continuation of the Grande Randonnée, the GR 21, and so is quite easy to follow. This stretch of coastline is again full of interest, and it is possible to follow the GR to Yport (12km.) or all the way to Fécamp (18km approx.), returning by bus – the Office de Tourisme at Étretat will give you details. En route you will pass the Aiguille de Belval, another stack, this time merely 40 m. high. Just beyond is the Valleuse du Curé, the scene of one of the adventures of Arsène Lupin. In this valley there is a tunnel through the cliff with steps heading down to a ledge above the beach – a perfect setting for a swashbuckling novel, but a journey only to be taken in reality by the most intrepid explorers. The tunnel was originally created for shrimp fishermen on the beach below. Farther along you pass the village of Vattetot and the deep wooded Valleuse de Vaucottes before reaching Yport.

If you would like just a short circular route including this stretch of coast, the Office de Tourisme at Étretat (opposite a small car park in the Place Maurice Guillard) can find you a small leaflet entitled *Falaises d'Étretat et charme du Pays de Caux*. This leaflet is a map of the area around Étretat on which 9 waymarked circuits have been drawn – a few words are included describing each village en route. Heading east along the cliffs, you can follow an 8km circuit passing the Aiguille de Belval and turning inland at the Valleuse du Curé. The way back then passes through the little village of Bénouville. The other circuits on this map are similarly well-waymarked on the ground, and you should have no trouble following any one of them. And if you want to venture farther afield, a comparable leaflet is produced by the Office de Tourisme at Fécamp.

Places of interest nearby

Étretat itself offers an assortment of diversions. If you are keen to learn more about the gentleman-thief Arsène Lupin, go along to the recently opened Clos Lupin in the Rue Guy de Maupassant. This is not a museum! Instead you are treated to interactive exhibits telling his adventures, swapping his identities and taking part in a treasure hunt. A series of concerts is held in the garden in summertime.

The farm of la Valaine was passed on the walk. This offers a 'presentation of the life of goats' and gives you the opportunity to taste – and buy – goats' cheese.

The Château Les Aygues in the Rue Jacques Offenbach was a one-time summer residence of the Queens of Spain. Set in wooded parkland, the furnishings are 19th century, with many souvenirs of the royal family. The château is open for one month of the year only, from mid-July to mid-August.

High on the Amont cliff is the Musée Nungesser et Coli. A museum with rather more space than exhibits, the story it tells is nevertheless interesting as well as tragic. On May 7th 1927, the aircraft Oiseau Blanc, with Nungesser as pilot and Coli as navigator, left Paris to attempt the flight to New York. That evening they were seen crossing the coast at Étretat. A couple of days later, a telegram was received from New York offering congratulations. Time passed before someone worked out there had been a mistake – the wrong plane had been seen landing. Soon it was realised the Oiseau Blanc had disappeared. The plane and its crew had vanished without trace – but they had been the 'first to dare'.

In July and August, the Train Touristique puffs its way thrice daily through the green valley between Étretat and Les Loges. An interesting variation on this is that you can make the return (downhill) trip by Vélo-Rail – a sort of bike-for-five that you pedal yourself along the rail tracks. Book for this at the station, off the Avenue Nungesser et Coli.

Fécamp, just up the coast from Étretat, is dominated by the Église de la Trinité. The church was built on the spot where a bottle said to be containing drops of Christ's blood from the Crucifixion was washed up from the sea. The original church was replaced by the present building in the 13th century. Magnificent it is, but you will need to go inside to see the best of it – high-vaulted nave, carved rood screens, medieval stained glass and more.

Fécamp is also renowned as the home of the liqueur Benedictine. In the early 16th century, Brother Vincelli began to distil a blend of herbs and spices in his monastery in the town. The amber liquid produced was said to have medicinal properties. The monastery was dissolved in the Revolution and the recipe disappeared – only to be miraculously found again in 1863 by Alexandre le Grand, a merchant of Fécamp. He called the liquid Benedictine – and there is now a vast and ugly Neo-Gothic Neo-Renaissance *Palais Bénédictine* to tell you all about it, with a host of art treasures thrown in for good measure.

23. Mills in the valley of the Durdent

Once upon a time, the Durdent valley rang with the sound of water-mills – although only two are still functional, many old ones remain on this peaceful riverside. Leaving the valley you climb to the agricultural plateau of the Caux, with wide views all around.

Grade: Moderate

Distance: 17km (10½ miles)

Time: 5 hours

Map: This route covers two maps, IGN Série Bleue 1809 E and 1909 O.

Start and finish: The church at Héricout-en-Caux

How to get there: Héricourt-en-Caux is 10km north of Yvetot, on the D131 at its intersection with the D149. There is parking in the square in front of the church.

Refreshment: There are just a couple of bar/restaurants in Héricourt-en-Caux. En route, there is a pleasant auberge at Le Hanouard.

Notes: This is an easy walk on good tracks and minor roads. There is only one significant gradient – the short climb out of the Durdent valley. Sturdy footwear is recommended, but trainers would do after a dry spell in summer. Carry drink and food with you – although resuscitation is possible about half-way round at le Hanouard (see above). And note that much of the route is exposed, so on a hot day, take appropriate sun-screening precautions.

Waymarking: Part of the route is on a Grande Randonnée and so is waymarked in white on red. Elsewhere the waymarking is yellow or blue – and it is sometimes less than obvious. Just follow the directions!

Introduction

Between the Seine and the channel is the region of the Caux, a limestone plateau topped with silt and clay. This is rich agricultural land, renowned for its dairy herds and for its crops of cereal, rape and flax. Through this plateau the River Durdent has cut a short and shallow furrow – just 23 kilometres of it between its source at Héricourt-en-Caux and the sea at Veulettes-sur-Mer. At one time this brief stretch of river was home to more than 60 watermills, all kept busy with the produce of the fertile fields above. The place was a hive of activity. Even today, two of the mills are still grinding the corn. The rest are in various states of repair, many converted to desirable residences and others still standing silently by the riverside.

There have been mills along the Durdent since Roman times. At one time the mills were in the possession of the landed gentry, but the Revolution saw an end to that privilege. In the 19th century, the new miller became an important man in village society, often a man of some learning. The mill was the place to strike deals and exchange gossip. There must have been plenty of tittle-tattling in the valley of the Durdent!

This walk passes several of the mills and plenty more can be seen across the valley on the other side of the river. Most have been converted, but the one at Oherville still has its wheel with paddles intact for you to see. At one point the route passes the soggy beds of

Old mill and water-wheel at Oherville

a water-cress farm in the low-lying fields beside the river. Farther on you reach le Hanouard, where the still-active flour-mill is beautifully preserved. From le Hanouard you climb to the plains of Caux above the valley, where the wide prairie of rippling corn extends to the horizon. In a green corner stands the Manoir d'Auffay, an impressive edifice with *murs polychromes* – patterned walls of multi-coloured brick and stonework, traditional in the Caux. Beside the manor is a fine dovecote, now the home of the 'Museum of dovecotes of the Caux'. Pigeon was a popular dish in these parts – and the birds were housed as stylishly as their owners. If you have energy when you return to Héricourt, you can seek out the source of the Durdent – the confluence of two streams beside the Moulin de Quetteville, on the outskirts of the town. Or you can take a few minutes to explore the church at the top of its 52 steps – it is modelled on the abbey-church at St. Martin de Boscherville, one of the few monastic establishments to survive the revolution.

The Walk

1. From the central square, climb the steps to the church, and walk around the right-hand side of it.. Take the road ahead, climbing uphill. After a few minutes walking, this road turns to a farm on the left, but you continue on the grassy track ahead. At the next cross-tracks, turn left and carry on across the field and into the woods. The pleasant track now descends to meet the main road.

2. Cross directly over the road to the Rue de Gréaume opposite. This road now takes you over the river beside a very fine house, which was obviously once a water-mill. About 100 metres on the far side, take the road to the right. You have now joined the Grande Randonnée, the GR 211, with white on red waymarks. After about 400 metres, the road goes off to a nature reserve, but you continue ahead on the obvious track. Soon you reach a road.

3. Cross over the road and take the track opposite, alongside the water-cress beds. The barbed wire barriers at each end can simply be lifted off the posts and replaced. The track continues under the trees and soon comes alongside a pretty stretch of river. Water-mills can be seen across the valley. Eventually you reach a road, the Rue des Moulins, and turn right.

4. At the junction, where the road to the right crosses the valley, keep straight ahead (leaving the Grande Randonnée). Soon you pass the 18th century Moulin d'Oherville with its wheel still in place. The road now leaves the river and climbs and then descends to the village of le Hanouard. At the junction with the calvary on your left, keep straight ahead. Soon you meet the main road at a junction where a half-timbered bar/restaurant stands on the corner.

5. Turn right on the road and cross the river – here you are on the GR 211 again. Cross the main road and take a track into the woods on the far side – opposite a most beautifully preserved and still functional mill. The track climbs quite steeply up the wooded slope and you emerge beside a wide prairie at the top. Here turn right and walk along the grassy track beside the field. White on red waymarks lead you on – but you can't really go wrong. At length you reach the handsome Manoir d'Auffay, hiding behind trees on the right. You have a better view of the dovecote further along at the entrance.

6. At the cross-roads beside the entrance to the manor, keep straight ahead on the Route du Manoir, signed to Oherville. At the next junction, in the village of Auffay, turn left on the Allée des Épines. Where this track goes to the left, continue ahead downhill on a hollowed out track under the beech trees on the left. Soon the track is running between fields on either side. At the point at which the track is about to enter the woodland, leave it and walk uphill along the edge of the field on the left. Waymarks are strangely absent. At the top of the hill, turn right on a track heading into the woods – it actually runs inside the woodland edge. This unlikely-looking track soon becomes wider – and GR waymarks appear again. The path descends to meet a tarmacked road. Turn right on this road, and, after about 50 metres, left on a

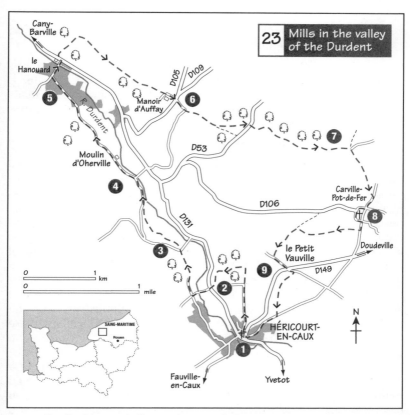

Cany-
Barville

le
Hanouard

5

R. Durdent

Moulin
d'Oherville

4

D105 D109

Manoir
d'Auffay

6

D53

7

Carville-
Pot-de-Fer

D106

8

D131

3

0   1 km
0   1 mile

le Petit
Vauville

Doudeville

9

D149

2

SAINE-MARITIME
Rouen

N

HÉRICOURT-
EN-CAUX

1

Fauville-
en-Caux

Yvetot

23   Mills in the valley
of the Durdent

path climbing uphill into the woods again. Continue on this broad
track along the edge of the woods for about 20 minutes to reach a
tarmacked road again.

7. At this junction, take the track to the right (leaving the GR). This
path bears a wooden signpost, *Chemin de Randonnée*. It leads you
uphill beside fields to arrive at a cross-roads in the village of
Carville-Pot-de-Fer. Here turn right and continue to the junction
with the D106, beside a calvary. Turn right on this main road, and
after about 150 metres, left on the Rue de l'Église. Pass in front of
the church, and continue to a junction with a wider road.

8. At this junction, turn right and in about 150 metres, turn right on
the Chemin de la Côte. This becomes a grassy track and continues
between fields. There appear to be no waymarks – although you
should be on a blue route. On reaching a tall hedge, continue
ahead with the hedge on your left. On the right there is first a pad-
dock and then another hedge. At the track T-junction, turn left on
a track heading towards a house surrounded by trees. Arriving at a
tarmacked road beside the house, continue ahead and reach a

T-junction – a *Chemin de Randonnée* sign greets you. Turn left and keep ahead to the main road.

9. Cross straight over the main road and take the Rue des Colombiers, which heads off to the left. About 250 metres along, take a track on the right, in front of a house. This grassy track leads up over the hill. Coming out at a main road beside a calvary, turn right and walk back down the hill into Héricourt-en-Caux.

More Walks in the Area

If you have never before taken a linear walk along a Grande Randonnée, the GR 211 between Héricourt-en-Caux and the sea at Veulettes-sur-Mer is an excellent stretch to begin on. The total distance is about 25km (15½ miles), but if you have taken the walk described, you will have already followed it as far as le Hanouard (approx. 6km.). Between here and the sea you will pass many more water-mills, and the fine 17th-century Château de Cany. The local tourist board have peppered the area with display boards describing local features of interest – several stand beside the route. Cany-Barville is about half-way along for a lunch stop – and you end appropriately enough on the long beach at Veulettes-sur-Mer. The route is well-waymarked with white on red flashes – all you need are two free leaflets, *Haute Vallée de la Durdent* and *Basse Vallée de la Durdent*, obtainable from the Office de Tourisme at Cany-Barville or Veulettes-sur-Mer. The route of the GR 211 is clearly marked on these leaflets (and it can be found on the IGN map or the Topoguide named below). You will also need transport one way. This is no problem if you have two cars, but otherwise ask the Office de Tourisme to help you find a taxi.

If Grande Randonnée walking suits you, there's much more information to be found in the Topoguide *Pays de Caux, Côte d'Alabâtre (Ref. 202).* Here the whole route of the GR 211 is given in detail along with that of several other Grandes Randonnées in this region. A truly splendid route is the GR 21, following the chalk-cliffed coast all the way from Le Havre to Le Tréport. Any section would make an excellent walk – see Walk 22 from Étretat.

If short circuits are more to your liking, the helpful Office de Tourisme at Cany-Barville should be able to find you a series of free leaflets showing all the waymarked circuits in the area – and there are many! The route of this walk was a compound of several on the leaflet entitled *Haute Vallée de la Durdent*, on which there are several more routes for you to try. The waymarking on the ground here seems a bit old (it may be renewed) but the map itself is quite clear. The minimal French text just tells you what there is to see en route. At least take the 30 minute stroll (starting from the church at Héricourt) to the source of the Durdent and the Moulin de Quetteville, shown in this leaflet.

Set out on the road to Yvetot and turn right between the garage and the pumping station – follow the yellow spots.

Places of interest nearby

For a complete tour of this interesting area, get the free leaflet *Vallée de la Durdent – Circuit de Découverte*. This describes a route of 50km (31 miles) taking you past a series of display boards giving local information. The route is almost all on minor roads and is intended for motorists or for cyclists – hiring a bike at Cany-Barville, it would make a splendid week-end tour.

The Musée des Colombiers Cauchois and the colourful Manoir d'Auffray are open every afternoon except Wednesday in July and August. The dovecote museum may also be open at weekends in June and September. If you want to pursue the fascinating dovecote theme – get a leaflet entitled *Route des Colombiers Cauchois* from the Office du Tourisme and take to the road.

The Château de Cany, on the road to Cany-Barville, is a large and impressive formal edifice built in the time of Louis XIII. Around the château is a moat fed by the waters of the Durdent, and inside is wealth of antique furniture. The château is open every day except Wednesday in July and August

At Cany-Barville, the Eco-Musée Saint-Martin is situated in the workshop of a 15th century mill. The mill itself and its workings are being restored. On display elsewhere are the workshops, crafts and tools of past centuries, the interior of a cottage, the old machines of the linen industry, toys of former times, old vehicles and more. It is open on weekday afternoons from April to October – and the occasional Sunday.

The River Durdent is really not so short. The distinction of being *le plus petit fleuve de France* allegedly belongs to a nameless river of 1.1km that arises behind the seaside town of Veules-les-Roses, just east of St. Valéry-en-Caux. Veules-les-Roses is a particularly pretty spot, and you can take a stroll around the whole river valley in under an hour. But the Tourist Office has added to the route a number of detailed information boards – so it will probably take you a little longer.

And finally, for curiosity value, take a short drive to see the Allouville Oak. It stands (with a little help) in front of the church at Allouville-Bellefosse, a village on the D34, south-east of Yvetot. This venerable old tree is said to be more than 1,200 years old! Way back in the 17th century two chapels were built in its trunk – an intrusion usually reserved for yew trees. That trunk is now 16 metres in circumference, and the branches arising from it are propped or suspended by some very Heath-Robinson looking contraptions. The tree has been ailing of late – go along now while there's time!

24. The Seine at Villequier

At Villequier the Seine tells a sad story, while upstream at
Caudebec-en-Caux pavement cafés cheerfully line its banks. This walk
explores the countryside between the two, with many fine views of the
river and the distant elegant Pont de Brotonne.

Grade: Moderate

Distance: 15km (9½ miles). A short cut reduces it by about 2km.

Time: 4½ hours walking

Map: IGN TOP 25.1911 OT

Start and finish: The Victor Hugo Museum at Villequier

How to get there: Villequier is on the right bank of the Seine, 4km
west of Caudebec-en-Caux. There is a small parking area for those
visiting the museum alongside the main road. Should this be full,
there is more parking about 500 metres along the road to
Caudebec-en-Caux at the riverside park.

Refreshment: There are a couple of bar/restaurants in Villequier,
while Caudebec-en-Caux offers an infinite variety of establishments,
many of them beside river.

Notes: This walk is all on very minor roads and well-defined field and
woodland tracks – but it does involve some climbing. The banks of the
Seine between Villequier and Caudebec-en-Caux are quite steep. For
footwear, walking boots would be preferable, although trainers would
get you by in dry weather. The route involves several stretches of
woodland and would be pleasant on a hot day – although there is also
an open section across farmland on the plateau of the Caux. Take
binoculars if you want to enjoy distant views of the river.

Waymarking: Much of the route is on Grande Randonnée, with
excellent white on red waymarking. The remainder is waymarked in
blue, with a short section in green – all is described in the text.

Introduction

At Villequier the sad statue of Victor Hugo looks out over the Seine –
where, in September 1843, his beloved daughter was drowned.
Léopoldine was merely 20 years old and recently married when she
and her husband Charles Vacquerie set out for a boating trip on the
river. The *mascaret* – the Seine bore – was the cause of the tragedy.
Both lost their lives and Hugo, who was devoted to his daughter, was
devastated. He poured his grief into poetry:

> Demain, dès l'aube, à l'heure où blanchit la campagne,
> Je partirai. Vois tu, je sais que tu m'attends
> ... Et quand j'arriverais, je mettrai sur ta tombe
> Un bouquet de houx vert et de bruyère en fleurs.

Les Contemplations is now considered to be one of his best works.
   The *mascaret* is no longer the tyrant of the Seine. It was once a fea-

ture of the high tides of the equinoxes, a huge breaking wave up to four metres high, travelling upstream at around 30 kilometres an hour. After the estuary of the Seine was dredged in the 60s, the dreaded *mascaret* was seen no more. The house of the Vacquerie family, on the riverside at Villequier, has now become a museum displaying some of Victor Hugo's letters, books and writings, family photographs and other memorabilia. Léopoldine, her husband and her mother (although not the great man himself) are all buried in the nearby churchyard.

This walk from Villequier climbs the steep wooded banks above the Seine and crosses a pleasant corner of open countryside to come down to the river again at Caudebec-en-Caux. There is a fine view of its Gothic church as you approach. In contrast to Villequier, Caudebec is a busy place – a town that makes much of its riverside with seats and children's games, mini-golf and gardens. A row of pavement cafés overlook the Seine – the ideal place to stop for lunch and be amazed by the sheer bulk of some of the vessels moving on the river. Just upstream, the Pont de Brotonne, built in 1977, spans the Seine with a certain French elegance. If you have time to spare, take a moment to look round the church – or visit the fascinating Musée de la Marine de Seine beside the river – before you set off again.

The homeward trail involves more climbing – but as you go, you pass a tiny mariner's chapel, an old château and one of those finely-balanced rocks that wobble at a touch, but never fall. Eventually you descend to Villequier, and from the slopes have a final opportunity to look along the length of the Seine to the now distant Pont de Brotonne.

The Walk

1. From the Musée Victor Hugo beside the river, walk directly up to the main road, passing through the little car park. At the main road, turn right, and in about 200 metres, take a road on the left (Rue President Rene Coty) leading uphill past the church where the Hugo family are buried. Just before reaching the church, turn right on a track heading up into the woods. The waymarking is that of a Grande Randonnée, white on red. The path climbs steeply with good views, and at the top of the slope, you reach a path junction with GR waymarks to the right. Ignore the waymarks, and keep ahead alongside a half-timbered house, between rows of conifers. Reaching the access road to the houses, follow it to the public highway.

2. Here turn left (leaving the Grande Randonnée), and at the road junction in about 150 metres, turn right. A similar distance brings you to another junction, where you turn left on the narrow Chemin de la Landrière. You can see the church at St Arnoult across the fields and the road soon bears right, heading towards it.

Blue waymarks appear and you will be following these for the next hour or so until you enter the forest.

3. Reaching the main road in St. Arnoult, cross over and take the road on the opposite side, just past the church. A signpost informs you that this is the start of the *Circuit Chamois* – but don't get confused – you want the blue circuit. Just up the road, one branch of the *Chamois* goes off on the left but you continue ahead with both blue and chamois waymarks. After passing a pond, look out for a turning taking you across fields on the right. Further on, at the corner of a field, turn right (the Chamois Circuit goes ahead here) and walk along the edge of the field with the church at St. Arnoult on your right. Soon your feet are on tarmac again and you descend to a road. Turn left and in about 100 metres, right, into the village of Houquetot.

4. In about 300 metres, at the T-junction with a farm on the left, turn left, but in a further 200 metres or so, turn right on a road signed to La Bouillotte. A road from the right joins, and you arrive at a cross-roads beside a water-tower. Cross straight over and continue on the road to the forest edge.

As the road enters the forest, take a track on the right going downhill. After about 150 metres on this stony track, branch off to the right uphill again, on a track leading to the forest edge. Now keep to the track along the edge of the forest, waymarked in blue – do not go down into the deep valley on the left. Eventually your track descends through the trees to meet a cross-track at the bottom of a hill.

Musée Victor Hugo

5. At this point you meet the green route and have the option to take a short cut. To take this, turn right, following both blue and green waymarks through the forest to arrive at Point 6 in about 15 minutes – you will have cut out about 2km of forest walk

To continue with the main route, turn left here, following green waymarks. After 7 or 8 minutes walking through the forest, the track begins to descend and you can see the village of Ste. Gertrude through the trees ahead. Here take a track doubling back on the right (it is well-concealed, so keep your eyes open), waymarked as a Grande Randonnée, white on red. This track soon brings you to the edge of the forest above the valley of the Ste. Gertrude River. After about half an hour, you have views down the valley to Caudebec-en-Caux with its prominent Gothic church. 10 minutes or so later, the track swings to the right away from the valley and shortly comes down to meet the main road at a hairpin bend. Turn right on this, and in about 100 metres, take an uphill gravelled track on the right, into the woods again.

6. Where the track bears right, leave it and take a path up the bank on the left, waymarked as a Grande Randonnée. Those who have

taken the short cut join again here. At the top of the hill this bears left and meets a tarmacked road. Turn left on this road and walk down to the main road. Cross straight over this to a track opposite. This descends through the trees and bears right to come down to another gravelled road. Turn right on the road (towards the bend) and in a few metres you have a choice.

7. If you want to avoid Caudebec-en-Caux completely, you can turn right here and follow the Grande Randonnée signs through the woods and down the bank to pick up this route at Barre-y-Va. But to visit Caudebec, keep ahead on the road. This is the spot known a Le Calidu – the site of a Roman hill-fort, with a fine view. Continue to some steps leading you on to the main road, and turn right here to reach the lively riverside at Caudebec. The Musée de la Marine de Seine is in front of you, and the church is up a road on the left. Shops and cafés are to the left along the river front and Tourist Information is at its far end.

   When ready to leave, take the road to Villequier, passing the museum. The road soon comes back beside the Seine, after which you take the first road on the right, signed to *Chapelle de Barre-y-Va*. Ten minutes walking will bring you to the chapel – an old mariner's chapel, built at the time of Louis XIV, which is usually open. Inside are model ships and other offerings presented by the sailors of the Seine in gratitude for being spared its perils. The site of the chapel is the hamlet of Barre-y-Va – meaning 'Bore comes here'. Continue along the road for a further 500 metres, to a fork in front of the gates of a house.

8. At this fork, take the right-hand track, uphill. This soon passes beneath some overhanging rock above which is balanced the rocking Pierre Tournante – it wouldn't be easy to test it! At another fork, go left, still following the white on red waymarks (the blue route goes straight ahead). The sunken track now climbs through dense woods. Eventually you reach the woodland edge, and then emerge at a tarmacked road beside a château with a view. Walk along the road, and just after the left-hand bend you arrive at Point 2 again, the end of the drive to the houses. Turn left here, then left between the conifers and retrace your steps to Villequier.

More Walks in the Area

Another very popular walk in these parts, again with both woodland and views of the Seine, starts from the magnificent Church of Notre-Dame in Caudebec-en-Caux.. The 10km route initially hugs the steep opposite side of the Ste. Gertrude valley. It then descends into the deep Val aux Meilles and returns through the woods to the fine viewpoint at la Vignette, from which sharp eyes can pick out the towers of the abbey at Jumièges, way upstream. The circuit is waymarked in yellow throughout (with a short section on GR) and can be found on the leaflet *De Seine en Forêts* as well as in the Topoguide *La Seine-Maritime à pied (Ref. D076)*

On the opposite bank of the Seine the ground is much flatter. Almost opposite Villequier is the interesting old village of Vatteville-la-Rue – the church has many maritime ex-votos (thanksgiving offerings) and the walls both inside and out bear the graffiti of mariners long gone. From the church, a 10km circuit leads you down to the towpath of the Seine – the best opportunity you'll get for a walk right beside it. Vatteville is also on the *Route des Chaumières* and there are many interesting old thatched cottages on the walk. The circuit is marked on the leaflet *De Seine en Forêts* and has also merited inclusion in the Topoguide mentioned above.

If you enjoy following Grandes Randonnées, which are always well-waymarked, a very easy and interesting circuit is possible from Caudebec-en-Caux. The IGN map mentioned above will help you sort it out – the GR is marked in red. Pick up the GR2 at the church at Caudebec and head up to the viewpoint at la Vignette. From there the route goes through woods and across the pretty valley of the Rançon, to reach St Wandrille-Rançon with its abbey. Leave the GR here and return alongside the Seine – not on the main road, but on another one parallel, marked in red on the map. The whole distance is about 10km.

And if this makes you keen to explore more of this Grande Randonnée, it runs the whole length of the Seine from Triel to Le Havre, a distance of 282 kilometres. It's all described in the Topoguide *La Seine en Normandie (Ref. 201),* including suggestions for day and weekend sections. This worthy Topoguide was once translated into English, but is now sadly out of print. Tackle it in French if you can – it offers lots of practical information.

Places of interest nearby

At Villequier, the Musée Victor Hugo is open every day except Tuesdays in winter. Quietly impressive with lots of memorabilia, it is inexpensive and well worth a visit. The statue of Victor Hugo contemplating the river is in the grassy park beside the road to Caudebec-en-Caux. Villequier was the spot where boats changed pilots heading up or down river – in its narrow streets and beside the river are several well-preserved old seamen's residences.

Caudebec-en-Caux was once the capital of the agricultural Caux region but its position was usurped by Yvetot. The town was almost completely destroyed by fire in the summer of 1940, but fortunately, the beautiful 15th century gothic-style church of Notre-Dame was unharmed. If you only have a moment, look at the carvings in the west doorway – 333 of them, their faces said to be modelled on those of the stone masons themselves. Inside are fine glass windows and much more, but it was surely the ornate exterior that caused Henry IV to exclaim that it was 'the most beautiful chapel in the kingdom'.

Down by the riverside, the Musée de la Marine de Seine will tell you everything you ever wanted to know about the river. You can even see the Seine bore in action, preserved for posterity on video. Old boats, fishing, ancient traditions, shipbuilding and the stories of those who made their lives on this river are interestingly displayed. The museum is open every afternoon except Tuesdays out of season.

Villequier and Caudebec-en-Caux are in the Brotonne regional park, whose headquarters are across the Pont de Brotonne at Notre-Dame de Bliquetuit. This is the place to go to get all possible information on the region – including walking routes (see Walk 25). If you fancy doing it on four wheels for a change, two driving routes start from the Maison du Parc. The first is the *Route des Fruits* along the bend of the river on which Jumièges is situated. Various fruit stalls are set out beside the orchards in season, and the route ends at *Le Monde merveilleux des abeilles* – an exhibition of beekeeping. The second route is the *Route des Chaumières*, along the Seine on the opposite side from Villequier. It passes many attractive thatched dwellings, typical of the region and you can visit Vatteville-la-Rue with its mariners church.

25. The Abbey of Jumièges

On a wide curve of the Seine below Rouen stand the elegant white ruins of
the Abbey of Jumièges. From the slopes above there are views of the river
on all sides as you take this walk through the woods in the Brotonne
Regional Park.

Grade: Easy / Moderate

Distance: 15km (9½ miles)

Time: 4½ hours

Map: IGN TOP 25 1911 OT

Start and finish: The Abbey of Jumièges

How to get there: From the D982, the road from Le Havre to Rouen,
turn south between the towns of Caudebec-en-Caux and Duclair (S.P.
to Jumièges). The abbey is in the centre of the small town and there is
parking opposite.

Refreshment: There are several bars and restaurants in Jumièges, and
a bar/crêperie en route at Mesnil-sous-Jumièges.

Notes: This walk is entirely on good tracks for which trainers would
be suitable footwear – at least in summer. The only possible
refreshment stop is at Mesnil-sous-Jumièges, about 10km into the
walk, so you might like to carry food and drink with you. Before
Mesnil-sous-Jumièges the route is wholly in woodland, but the last few
kilometres are in the open – sun-screen may be needed on a hot day.

Waymarking: This route is a compound of several waymarked
circuits. The initial dark blue marks are followed by the white on red
of a Grande Randonnée (points 2 – 4). After this, more dark blue,
then green and light blue marks lead you home. Don't worry – it's all
described in the text.

Introduction

Around Rouen the Seine embarks on a series of wide convolutions,
almost doubling the length of its journey to the sea. Resulting from this
are successive interlocking spurs of land, each one of which is almost
surrounded by the meandering river. On one of these promontories
stands the town of Jumièges. Its site is that of a monastic community
founded by St. Philibert in the 7th century, but the abbey you see
today was begun some 400 years later. Present at its consecration was
William the Conqueror, jubilant after his recent triumphs in England.
Of all the many abbeys of Normandy, Jumièges must surely have been
the most beautiful. It is still exquisite as a ruin, its twin octagonal
towers reaching high into the sky above a long nave and aisles with rib
vaulting. At the far end a single wall of the lantern tower still stands
high above an arch of impressive proportions. Originally a Benedictine foundation, the monastery was dissolved in the Revolution, and
subsequently sold at auction. Its purchaser was an enterprising timber

merchant – who, envisaging it as a ready-made stone quarry, employed dynamite. Rescued by a philanthropic family in the 19th century, it now belongs to the state. The site comprises the remains of two churches and the more recent Abbot's lodging house, now a museum. All are in white stone, on a sunny day making a striking contrast to bright green lawns and blue sky. The abbey is a popular tourist attraction – the car park opposite seethes with cars and coaches on a summer's afternoon. So make your visit early, before setting out on this splendid walk around the promontory.

Jumièges is in the Regional Natural Park of the Brotonne, an area of natural beauty taking in the forests and marshland along the banks of the tortuous Seine. Behind the town, the higher ground is clad with oak, beech and pine – the Forêt de Jumièges. The tracks of this forest – and of the others in the region – have been incorporated into an amazing number of colour-coded waymarked circuits of varied lengths. All you need is a free map from the local Tourist Office and off you go for a couple of month's walking! Having so many routes to choose from makes life complicated, but if you start with this one (an amalgam of several waymarked circuits) you will at least have a good idea of the area. And hopefully you will want to try out others.

The route starts beside the Abbey of Jumièges. From there it quickly climbs into the forest and crosses the spur of land to emerge high above the Seine on the other side. The splendid forest track now follows above the bank of the river and through the trees you can cast your eye on barges chugging their way through the water below. Eventually you descend to river level and pass the prolific orchards of Mesnil-sous-Jumièges. The village is on the 'Route des Fruits' – presumably the fruit trees are thriving on centuries of silt laid down by the river on its bend. The bar/crêperie offers welcome resuscitation before you make the journey home – on a route no longer through the forest, but still with distant sightings of the river and the white cliffs of its opposite bank.

The Walk

1. With the abbey on your right, walk up the road for about 100 metres and then take the next road on the right, which climbs uphill. At the cross roads in a further 100 metres or so, keep straight ahead, now following both light and dark blue waymarks. Passing the camping site (Camping de la Forêt), you come to a junction where the road you are on swings to the right. Waymarks of various colours are all round you. Leave the 'main' road here and keep straight ahead – the waymarks are now dark blue joined by the white on red of a Grande Randonnée. After a few hundred metres, the roads bends to the left (a track continues ahead into the forest). Keep with the road, which becomes a track and runs parallel to the forest edge across the fields.

2. At a cross-tracks in about 300 metres, turn right and head for the forest, now following only the white on red waymarks of the Grande Randonnée. The path at first climbs through mixed woodland and then flattens out along the summit. At a clearing, you come across a tiny chapel and a cross – this is apparently the place where Christ and his apostles appeared to Saint Philibert. Farther on you reach the Fosse St. Philibert, an earthen wall dyke that once defended this promontory. Soon you reach the forest edge and continue between fields for about 100 metres to a track junction.

3. Here you join another Grande Randonnée, the GR 2, doubling back to the right. A sign tells you this is a *sentier historique*, leading you to the Manoir Agnès Sorel and the Abbaye de Jumièges. Being a Grande Randonnée, the path is again well-waymarked in white on red, and you have no difficulty following it along the cliff edge high above the Seine. After half an hour or so of walking along this path, you meet a sign board telling you that this is the site of the *ligne funiculaire* where logs were taken down to the river at the time of the First World War. After passing through a pine plantation, the path begins to descend and on the left-hand side, you find a wooden gate, marked with a blue dot.

4. Turn left through the gate and walk downhill with some good views of the Seine from the sunken path. The waymarking is now blue. On reaching the road at the bottom, turn right (note the apple orchards – this is the Route des Fruits) and continue into the village of Mesnil-sous-Jumièges. A bar-crêperie greets you as you reach the main road.

5. Turn right here on the Rue de l'Église. Half-way up the street, the blue waymarks invite you to turn right, and a sign tells you that this way there is a panorama. Take it if you like – the panorama is merely a distant view of the Seine, but the much nearer church looks quite picturesque from here. Once seen, it is probably best to return to the Rue de l'Église and continue uphill to the T-junction (although turning left and left again will bring you to the same point). At the T-junction, turn left into the Rue de la Vigne, now again following Grande Randonnée waymarks to reach the main road .

6. Turn right on the road and follow it as far as the entrance to the *Base de plein air et de loisirs*. Turning in here, you come to a signpost bearing a green spot – you are temporarily on a green circuit. Now turning right, the path leads you past the camping site and then bears left to the edge of the lake. Reaching the shore, bear right to meet the road. At the road, turn right, and at its junction with the main road, cross straight over.

7. At the top of the road you meet the light blue dots again and con-
    tinue ahead. At a sharp left hand corner, take the stony and grassy
    track going straight ahead. There are wide views across to the
    Seine on the left. At the first cross-tracks keep straight ahead, and
    at the subsequent fork, bear right over the hill. The track leads up
    to a fine thatched cottage, which you pass on your right. A track
    now leads you on and over a road, still following light blue
    waymarks.

8. At a cross-tracks in front of another house, turn left. This
    cross-field track eventually brings you down to another road,
    where you turn right. There are now both light blue and green
    waymarks. Passing a rear entrance to the abbey, you arrive at the
    cross-roads you passed at the start of your journey. Turn left and
    then left on the main road to return to the Abbey.

More Walks in the Area

The key to walking in this part of the world is the acquisition of two
free leaflets – *De Seine en Vergers* and *De Seine en Forêts*. These can
be found in any local Office de Tourisme. The many routes shown are
as well waymarked on the ground as they are on the maps. There
should be problems only for the colour-blind! But which routes to
choose from so many? The route described here is largely a forest walk
– and there are plenty more of those on the leaflets. If you now want
something different, try the 15km loop *La Chapelle du Bout du Vent*
from the *Seine en Forêts* leaflet – not for the chapel, but for the 9km or
so stretch beside the banks of the Seine. The route starts just across the
river from Jumièges. Take the ferry (*le bac*) – an experience in itself.

   Again for something different, the Topoguide *La Seine-Maritime à
pied* describes a 10km route north of the Seine in the deep wooded
valley of the River Austreberthe. Along with beautiful countryside,
you will pass châteaux, an ancient chapel, a Roman camp and an old
water mill. The route starts from St. Pierre-de-Varengeville – and if
you don't want to invest in a Topoguide (pricey but interesting) you
can work it out from the *Seine en Vergers* leaflet. ·From St. Pierre-de-Varengeville, walk north to join the pink route, which takes
you across the river beside the mill. Where pink joins green, head
north on green, and then south to its junction with dotted red. Continue to follow dotted red in an anti-clockwise direction, and then
pick up yellow to return to St. Pierre-de-Varengeville. It all makes
sense when you see the map.

   For those who enjoy a linear walk, the 18km section of the GR 2 between Jumièges and the still inhabited Abbey of St. Wandrille will
make a good day's excursion. The route is almost entirely through forest, high above the banks of the Seine, passing the towns of Yainville
and Le Trait, where resuscitation is possible. Arm yourself with the appropriate IGN map (see above), on which the Grandes Randonnées
are shown in red, or go for the Topoguide La Seine en Normandie

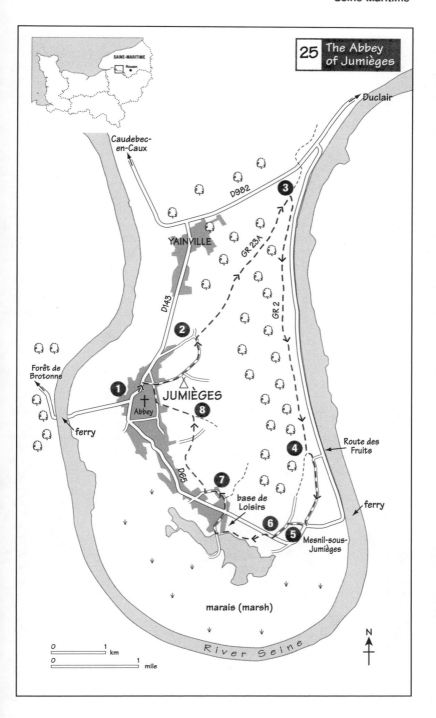

25 The Abbey of Jumièges

(Ref. 201), which has more information but manages to be a little confusing round here. It is possible to take the bus between Jumièges and St. Wandrille, or you could engage a taxi – enquire at the Office de Tourisme for both.

Places of interest nearby

There were many abbeys alongside the Seine, and one of the finest still standing is to the east of Jumièges at St. Martin de Boscherville. It's a mere 10km away as the crow flies, but an 18km drive around the meanders of the river (although with the aid of a map and two ferries you could walk it). The abbey here was spared the usual fate of such buildings in the Revolution by being adopted as the parish church. The Église St. Georges dates from around 1100 and is one of the best examples of Norman Romanesque architecture to be found. Another nearby abbey is that of St. Wandrille, near Caudebec-en-Caux. Built originally in the 7th century, it was ill-fated from the start, being frequently sacked by marauding Norsemen, burned to the ground and finally demolished when its spire collapsed. After the Revolution it became a spinning mill. Other owners followed, but in the 1930s the Benedictines bought back their birthright, took over the abbey site and set up their new church in a barn. Now these old walls again echo to the sound of Gregorian chant – and the abbey welcomes visitors.

The *Parc Naturel Régional de Brotonne* offers lots of interest. To obtain more information, go along to the *Maison du Parc* at Notre-Dame de Bliquetuit, just south of the Brotonne bridge. This is an outing in itself – the headquarters occupies an old farm with extensive grounds and outbuildings. There are picnic facilities, exhibitions – and lots of literature to guide you around the region.

Chapel in a yew tree at La-Haye-de-Routot

Natural Regional Parks seek to encourage traditional crafts, and the village of la-Haye-de-Routot, on the edge of the Brotonne forest is worth a visit. From Jumièges, take the ferry, which crosses every half hour (with the usual extended French lunchbreak) and head west through the forest. La-Haye-de-Routot sports a bread oven producing traditional bread and a clog-maker's workshop. Most fascinating are two very old trees in the churchyard – one houses a shrine, but, almost to outdo its neighbour, the other has a complete chapel within its trunk. For other interesting places in the Park, see Walk 24 from Villequier.

26. Chalk Cliffs at Criel

Near Criel, the sheer white cliffs fall over 100 metres to the pounding sea below. This is a bracing walk along the tops, with fine views to sea, and from the heights of Mont Jolibois, a coastal panorama extending all the way to Picardy.

Grade: Moderate

Distance: 10km (6¼ miles). A short cut will reduce the distance by 4km.

Time: 3 hours for the whole route.

Map: IGN Série Bleue 2000 E. But the map leaflet mentioned in the More Walks section is quite adequate – and free.

Start and finish: The Manoir de Briançon at Criel-sur-Mer

How to get there: Criel is about 10km south of Le Tréport, just north of the D 925. From Le Tréport, leave the D 925 at the roundabout (SP Criel.) Head into town, and after passing the road sign-posted to Criel-Plage (on the right), take the next turning on the right to reach the big car park in front of the Manoir de Briançon. (If you cross the river bridge you have gone too far)

Refreshments: There are several restaurants and cafés in Criel (Bourg) and a Pizzeria with a sea view in Criel-Plage.

Notes: This walk is suitable for trainers on a summer's day, but note that the grass on the cliff-tops is long in places, and will be wet after rain. The path is generally well set back from the cliff edge – do not be tempted to get a closer look! You should be particularly watchful of children on the cliffs. If the sun is shining, remember that there is no shade on most of the route, so make sure you have protection. And if you fancy a dip in the sea, bathing is possible at Criel-Plage, but the beach is shingly and quite steeply shelving.

Waymarking: The path along the cliff is a Grande Randonnée, waymarked in white on red. Elsewhere the route is waymarked in yellow.

Introduction

Between Le Tréport and Le Havre, the 120km of white-cliffed shore has rather fancifully been dubbed the Côte d'Alabâtre – the Alabaster Coast. In some ways it seems an appropriate name, since there are places along this coast where the limestone cliffs seem to have been carved by divine hand into fairy-tale arches and pointed pillars. Not so at Criel. Here the cliffs simply fall abruptly to the ocean below, their white faces apparently cut by a giant spade – or perhaps bitten by giant teeth to account for the jagged edges. At over 100 metres tall, these are said to be the highest cliffs in France. It must be said that the same claim is made for the granite cliffs at the Nez de Jobourg (see Walk 2) – but their sloping gorse-clad faces put them in a different league. This is a walk along the edge of a precipice and it is an exhilarating experience.

The walk starts from the town of Criel at the foot of a high ridge known as Mont Jolibois. Criel-sur-Mer is a town in two parts – Criel Bourg and Criel-Plage are separated by a couple of kilometres of narrow road. In Criel Bourg is found the beautiful 16th century Manoir de Briançon, now housing the municipal offices, standing on a picturesque site beside the River Yères. From here the route climbs through woods on the slopes of Mont Jolibois to emerge with a fine view of the coast. The sea is then in view all the way – at first at a distance, but after passing the little hamlet of Mesnil-à-Caux, right below you. As you walk along the high cliffs you can hear the sea beneath churning on banks of shingle ground from the rockface. At one point you dip into a deep dry valley before climbing finally to reach the viewpoint on the edge of Mont Jolibois. Here you look down over the pebble beach of Criel-Plage where the River Yères runs out to the sea. Along the coast the white cliffs go on, and on a fine day you can see the promontory at the mouth of the River Somme and beyond it, the coast of Picardy. It's a perfect spot for a picnic – but if you want the refinement of a table, you will have to return to the riverside site of the Manoir de Briançon, where you will also find a display board describing other walks in the pleasant valley of the Yères.

The Walk

1. From the car park, walk in front of the Manoir and take the path between the main building and the toilet block.(waymarked in yellow on red here – the waymarking of a GR du Pays). This path soon crosses the River Yères on a wooden bridge and then continues to a road. Cross this road directly and continue on the Rue des Érables. Passing a junction with a multitude of signs, keep straight ahead to a T-junction.

2. At this T-junction, turn right on the Chemin de la Cavée. The waymarking is now yellow. The track soon begins to climb quite steeply through woods of oak and beech on the flank of the ridge called Mont Jolibois. Just before the summit, you reach a fork where you keep to the left. Soon the path begins to descend and then emerges from the trees with a glorious view across country to the sea ahead. The fields are cultivated – this is the rich agricultural land of the plateau of Caux. The wide and now grassy path continues downhill curving to the left and you reach a track junction at a sharp left-hand corner.

3. The path ahead is the short cut and will take you directly to the coast, cutting about 4km off the route.

   To continue with the main walk, keep to the track bearing to the left. Now you skirt a field for aeromodelling enthusiasts, and after-

The Manoir de Briançon

wards, at the track junction, turn left, away from the sea. The road soon corners to the right and descends towards a village at the bottom of the hill. Following the yellow waymarks, keep ahead at a fork of tracks and then eventually join the road into the village of Mesnil-à-Caux.

4. At the road junction in the village, yellow waymarks go both ahead and to the right to confuse you! The route chosen for this walk turns right on the Rue du Calvaire. This leads you past the pond and calvary in the village. Through the village, the road forks – the track ahead goes down to the sea, but you bear right following the yellow waymarks. As you descend, it seems the track ahead is barred by wire. Do not worry – as you reach the wire you can see a narrow path going left towards the sea, marked by yellow flashes. Descending steeply on this path, you pass a stile on the left and continue almost to the edge of an inlet in the cliff.

5. Here you turn right on to the clifftop, now following the white on red marks of the GR 21. The path is obvious and you can simply enjoy the views of cliff and sea, the seagulls in the air and the wild-flowers of the clifftop at your feet. After something like half an hour, you come to the point where the short cut joins the cliff path, and soon afterwards, arrive at the Val Pollet. Here there are steep ladders down into the valley and up again on the other side. From here you cross a squeeze style and bear left, now keeping a fence between you and the cliff edge. Three fields are crossed in succession, keeping to the left in the first two and heading across the middle of the third. At the far side you turn uphill and cross the final squeeze stile at the top. This is the viewpoint on Mont

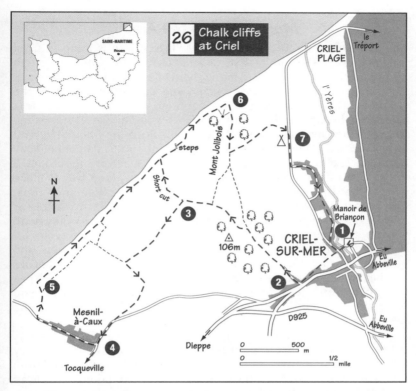

Jolibois – Criel Plage is way below you, the next town on the coast is Mesnil-Val and the distant views then go on to the mouth of the Somme and Picardy.

6. When you have taken in the view, turn right on a track leading into a shrubbery of blackthorn. Winding through the bushes, the track arrives at a T-junction, where you turn left, still following the waymarks of the Grande Randonnée. The track descends with good views of Criel Plage, and reaches a tarmacked road, the D 222, beside a camping site.

7. Turn right along the road, and at the end of the camp site, turn left on Basse Rue. Where this road corners right, two paths leave on the left. The first is the route of the Grande Randonnée – but you leave this now, and take the second path, keeping the beautiful ornamental garden on your left. The path is now waymarked in yellow again. Emerging between walls, you arrive at a tarmacked road with the river on your left, and continue ahead, following the waymarks. At the main road, turn left, and in about 100 metres, opposite the Rue des Érables, turn left again and retrace your steps over the Yères to the Manoir de Briançon.

173

More Walks in the Area

The tiny Office de Tourisme at Criel-Plage (there is none in Criel Bourg) is crammed with leaflets of attractions throughout the length and breadth of Normandy. Among them you should find a series of small maps showing walking, cycling and equestrian routes in the region of Criel – the walking leaflet is entitled *Vallées de l'Yères et de la Bresle – Chemin Vert du Petit Caux*. This last is very interesting. Between the town of Eu and St. Quentin-au-Bosc, the Chemin Vert du Petit Caux is a 17km grassy track following the route of an old railway line. The leaflet hastens to assure you that it is never monotonous! Those who established this route have gone out of their way to make sure of that by providing display panels describing flora and fauna, and a large wooden picnic shelter with more information at Touffreville. .The route itself is attractive, crossing several valleys with viewpoints from a viaduct and from the bridges of Touffreville, St. Sulpice and Eu. The wooded banks are rich in wild flowers and autumn adds another dimension with its profusion of blackberries and hazelnuts. The route is a little too long to walk there and back in a day and unfortunately there is no connecting public transport. If you have two cars there is no problem – otherwise, you could ask the Office de Tourisme in Eu to help you out with a taxi.

The leaflet named above maps out 12 circular walks in the valleys of the Yères and the Bresle between Criel and Le Tréport. There is very little text on this leaflet – the routes are intended to be followed from the map alone, with the aid of the excellent waymarking. This is all interesting country for walking, but if you want something different, try the 11km route in the Forest of Eu, starting from Incheville in the valley of the Bresle. This fine oak and beech forest is home to a large herd of deer and is particularly magnificent in autumn colours. There are several interesting forest sites such as the *pierre bise*, a druidic stone that steams after rain.

Two long distance routes are also shown on this map leaflet – the coastal path, the GR 21 and the Grande Randonnée du Pays, which makes a huge circuit including the valleys of both rivers. Both these routes are well-waymarked on the ground and it should be quite possible to follow a section of either of them using this little map. Transport is more difficult. There is a bus service between Le Tréport and Gamaches (approx. 24km by GRP), but elsewhere, it's two cars or a taxi.

Places of interest nearby

Just a few kilometres up the coast is the fascinating town of le Tréport at the mouth of the River Bresle. A popular seaside resort with Parisiens at the turn of the last century, it still attracts its holiday crowds. There is an interesting Old Town area which you can tour on foot or by train in summer and a leg-aching climb up some 350 or so steps (from the Hôtel de Ville) to a splendid viewpoint known as Les Terraces. A curious diversion is the wealth of ceramic wall plaques, dating from the town's heyday a hundred years or so ago – the local Office de Tourisme has devised a-family observation game on them, with a prize for those who spot them all. Le Tréport also makes the most of those chalk cliffs, illuminating them by night and offering boat trips to view them from the sea by day The same vessel takes fishing trips where you are taught the techniques and then invited to share the catch.

A couple of kilometres up the River Bresle from le Tréport is the old town of Eu. The 12th century Collegiale Notre-Dame et Saint-Laurent is one of the earliest examples of the Norman Gothic style. Not far away is the Château d'Eu, an edifice dating from the 16th century whose role is now both Town Hall and Musée Louis-Philippe. There are pleasant gardens with azaleas and rhododendrons – and being beside the forest, beech trees.

This may not be the appropriate place to mention it, but this area has some excellent waymarked cycle routes. Go to any Office de Tourisme and they can offer you free map leaflets – and tell you where to hire a bike (the leaflets tell you that anyway). The 36km coastal ride between Dieppe and le Tréport visits many seaside villages (and a nuclear power station). With extensions as far as Fécamp, it is said to be part of a European project for a cycle-route from The Netherlands to Portugal. Having less grand ambition, the simple circuit in the valley of the Yères (47km.) will make a good day's excursion – and for those less accustomed to the saddle, on the same leaflet there is an easier circuit of 25km with the hopefully not misleading appellation 'Vélo-Relax'!

In the same series:

Each book costs £9.95 (*Dordogne is just £8.95*) and contains a superb range of walks.

Available through all booksellers or direct from:
SIGMA LEISURE, 1 SOUTH OAK LANE, WILMSLOW, CHESHIRE SK9 6AR.
Phone: 01625-531035 Fax: 01625-536800.
E-mail: info@sigmapress.co.uk
Web site: http//www.sigmapress.co.uk